Luiz Moises
2024

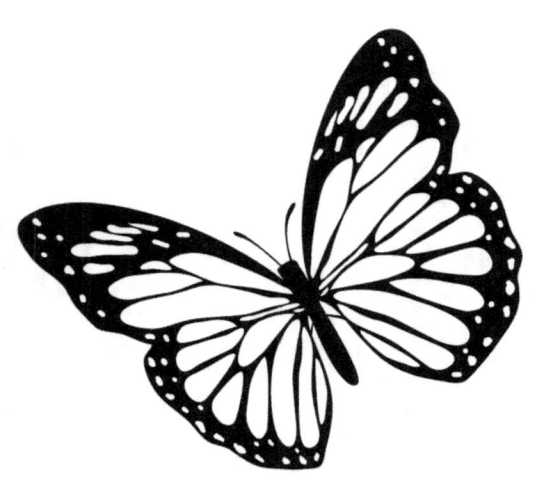
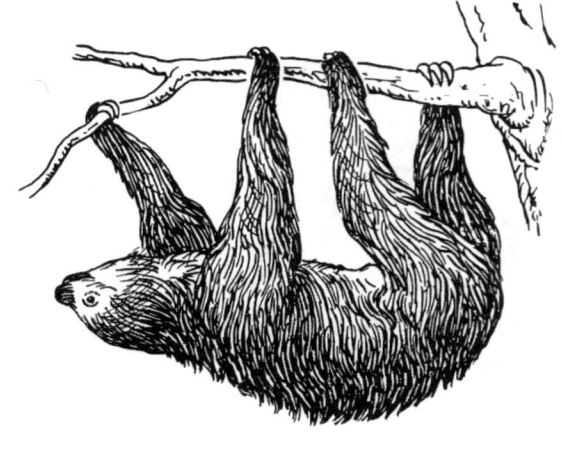

WHOSE BOOK IS IT:

○────────────────────────────────○

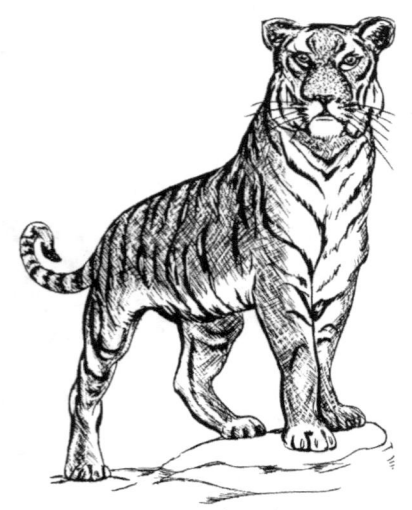
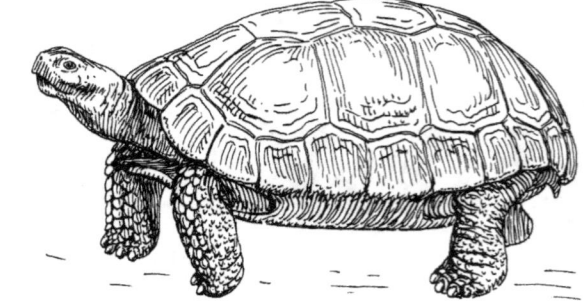

ALL RIGHTS RESERVED©

None of this publication may be reproduced, distributed, or transmitted in any form or by any means, including photocopying, recording, or other electronic or mechanical methods, without the prior written permission of the publisher, except in the case of brief quotations embodied in critical reviews and certain other noncommercial uses permitted by copyright law. Any unauthorized reproduction of this work is prohibited.

LMP©
LUIZ MOISES

COLOR TEST

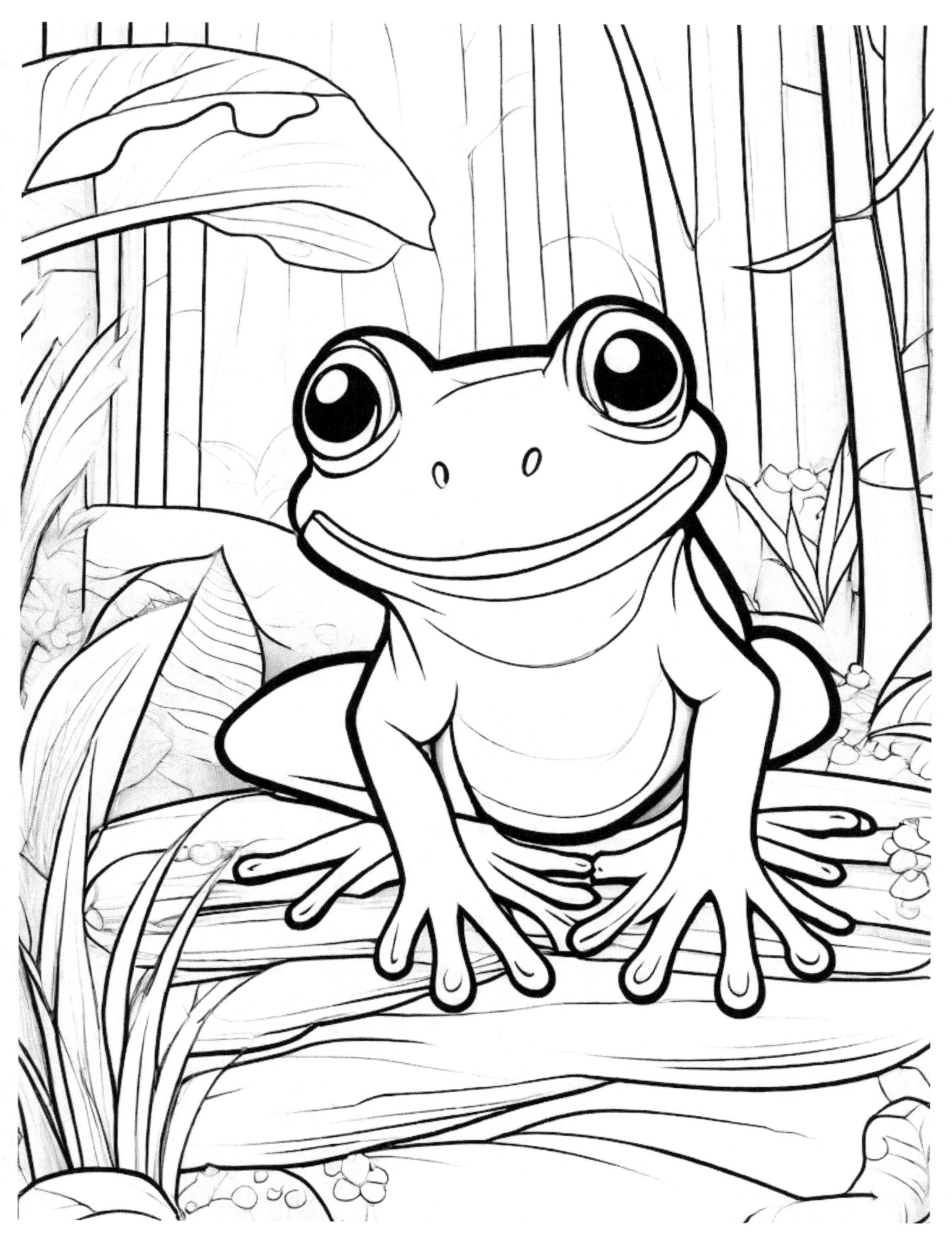

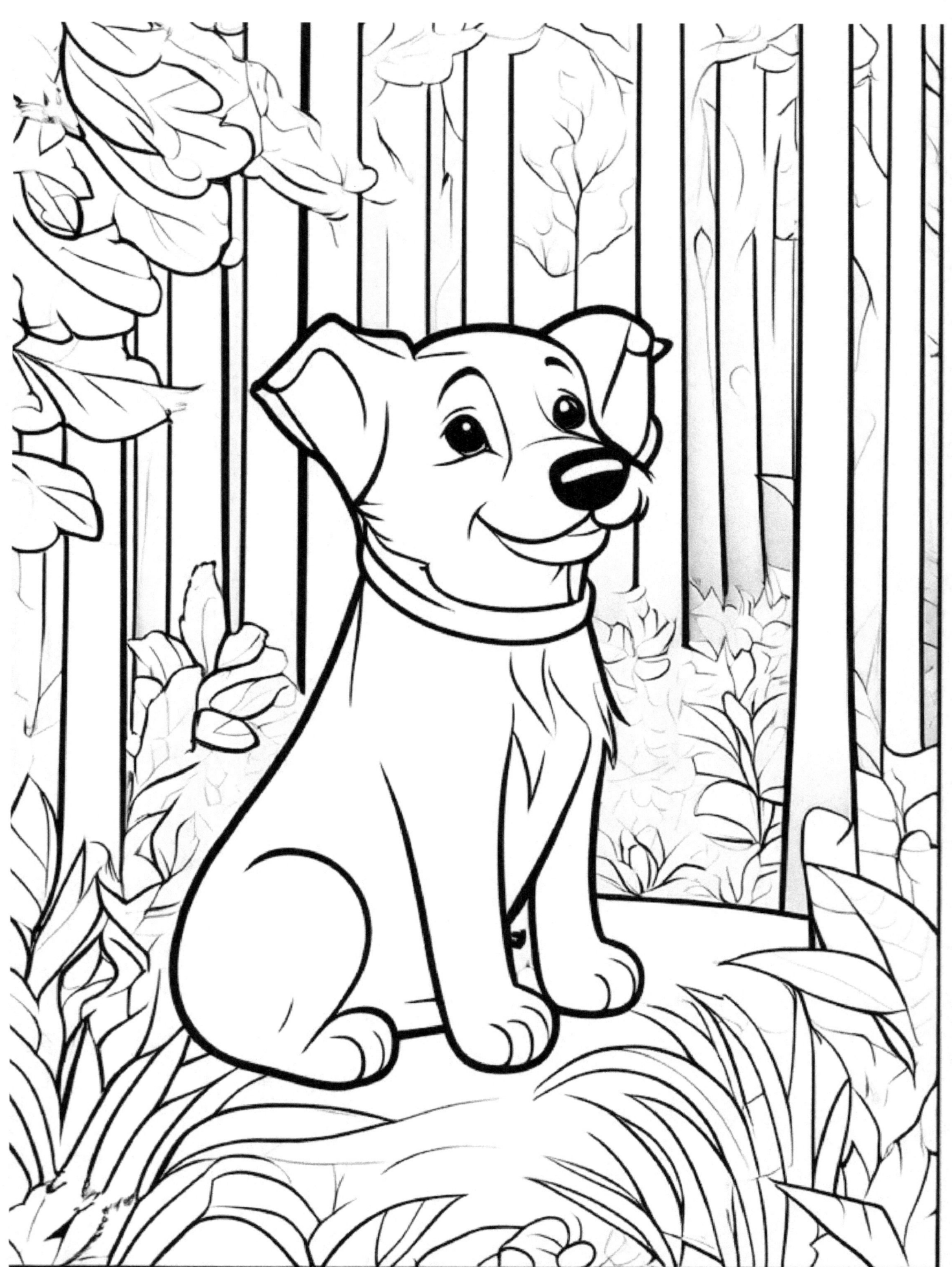

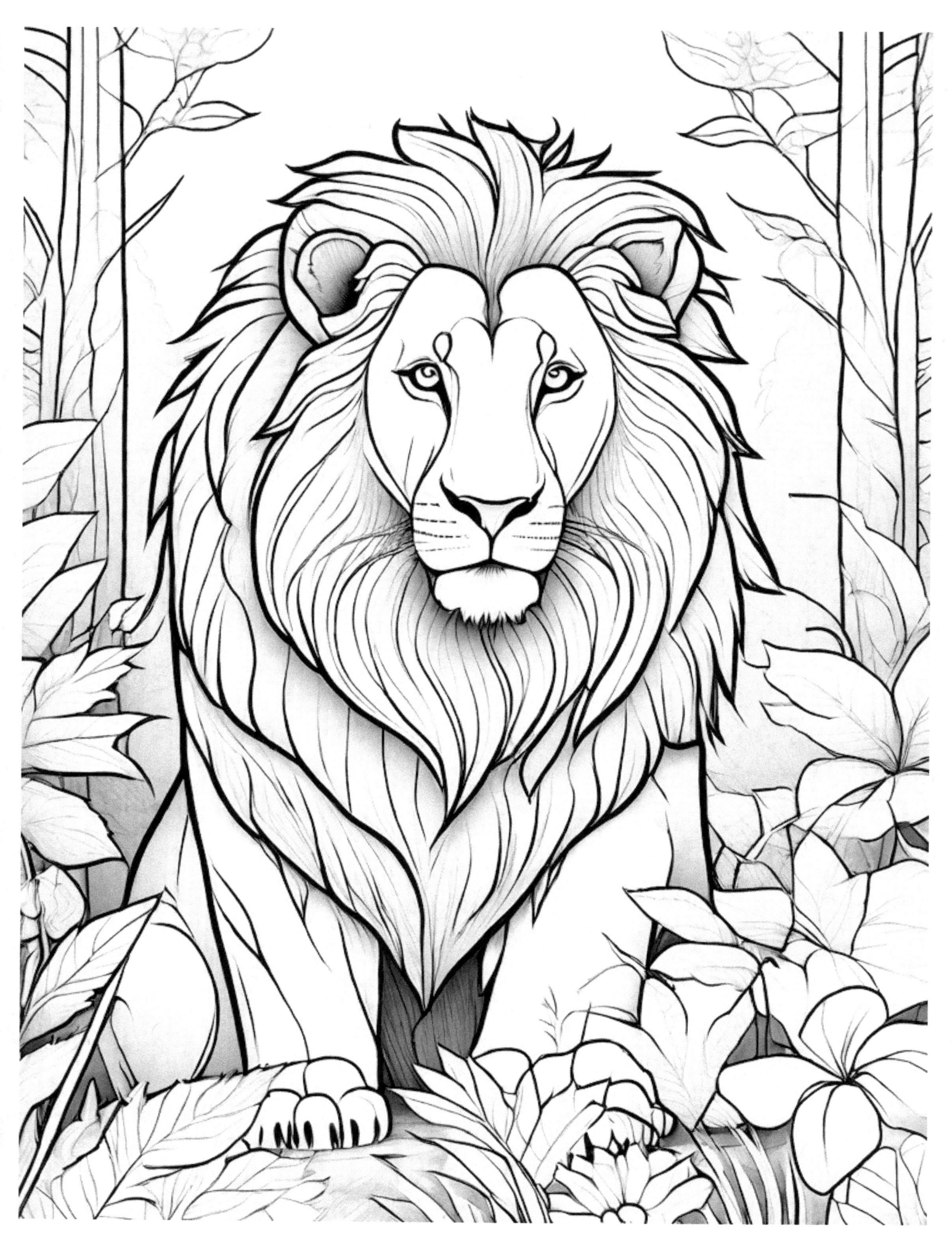

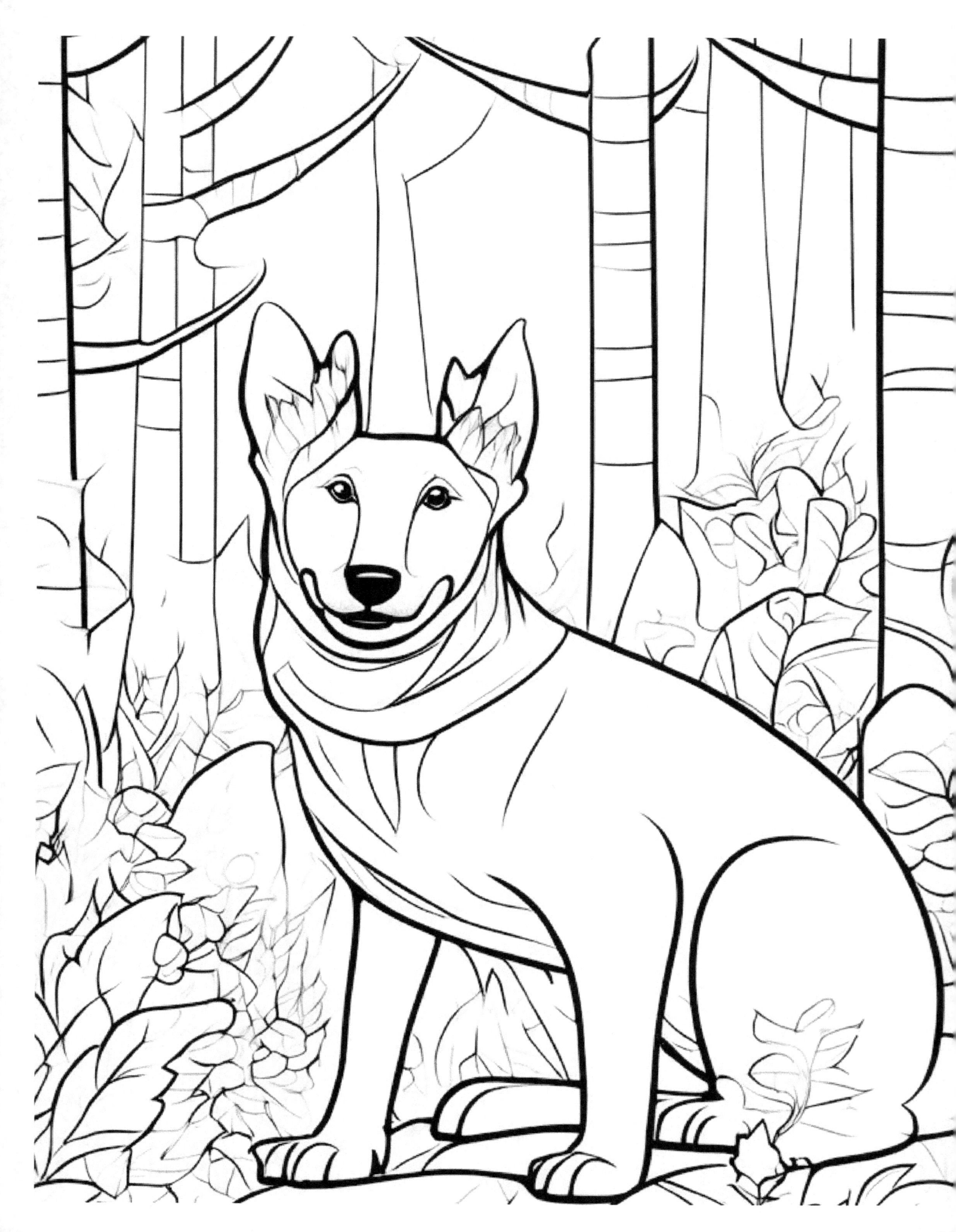

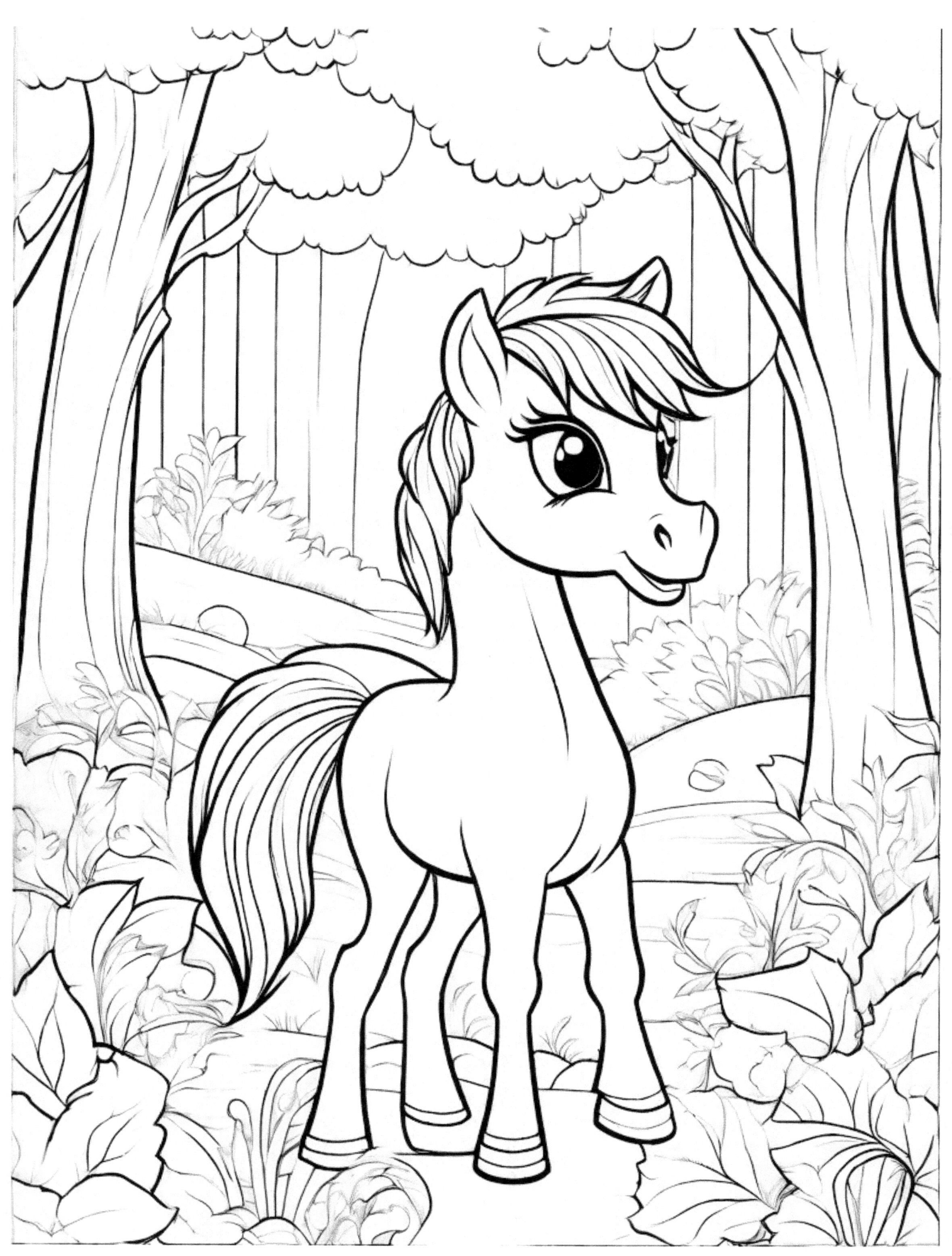

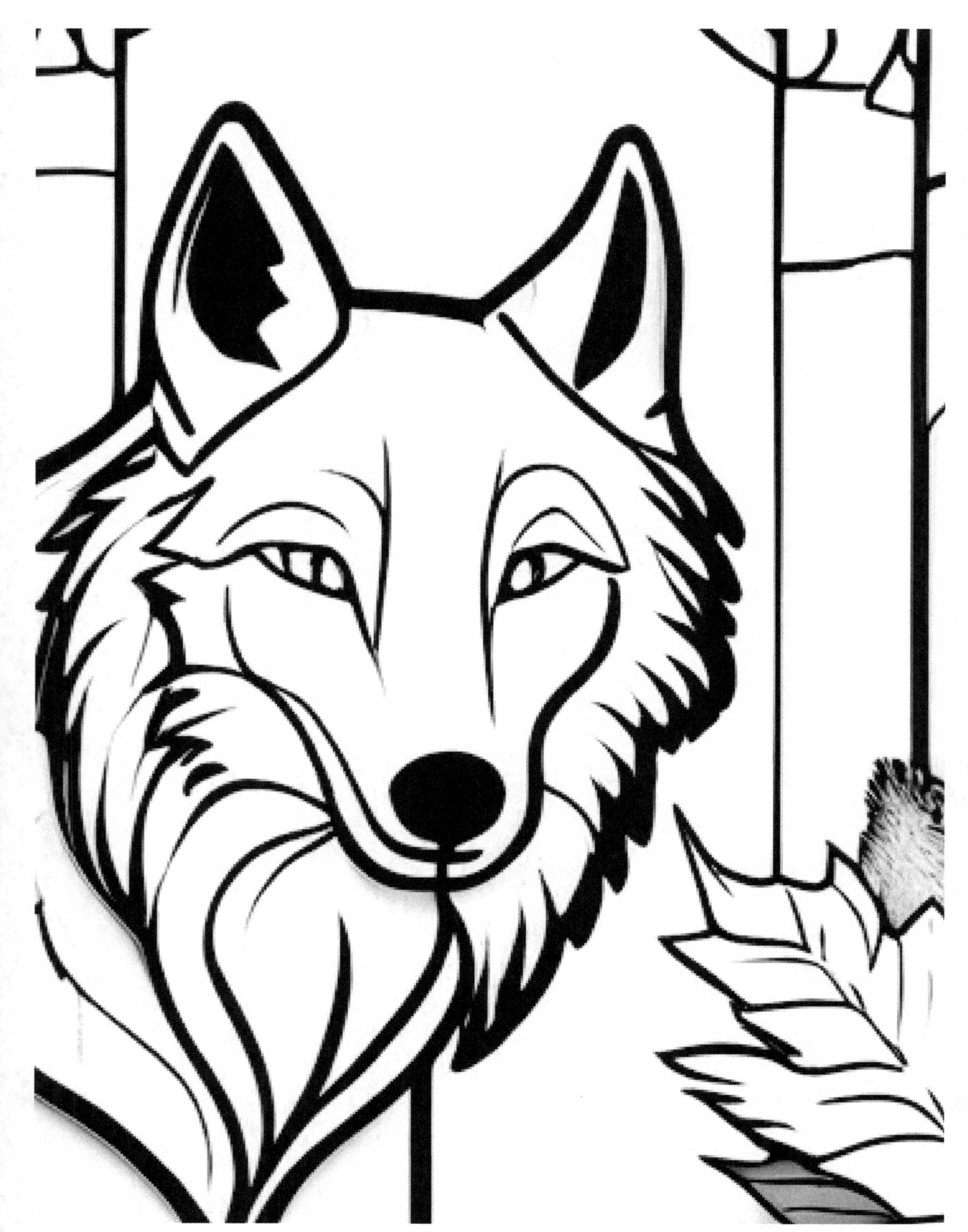

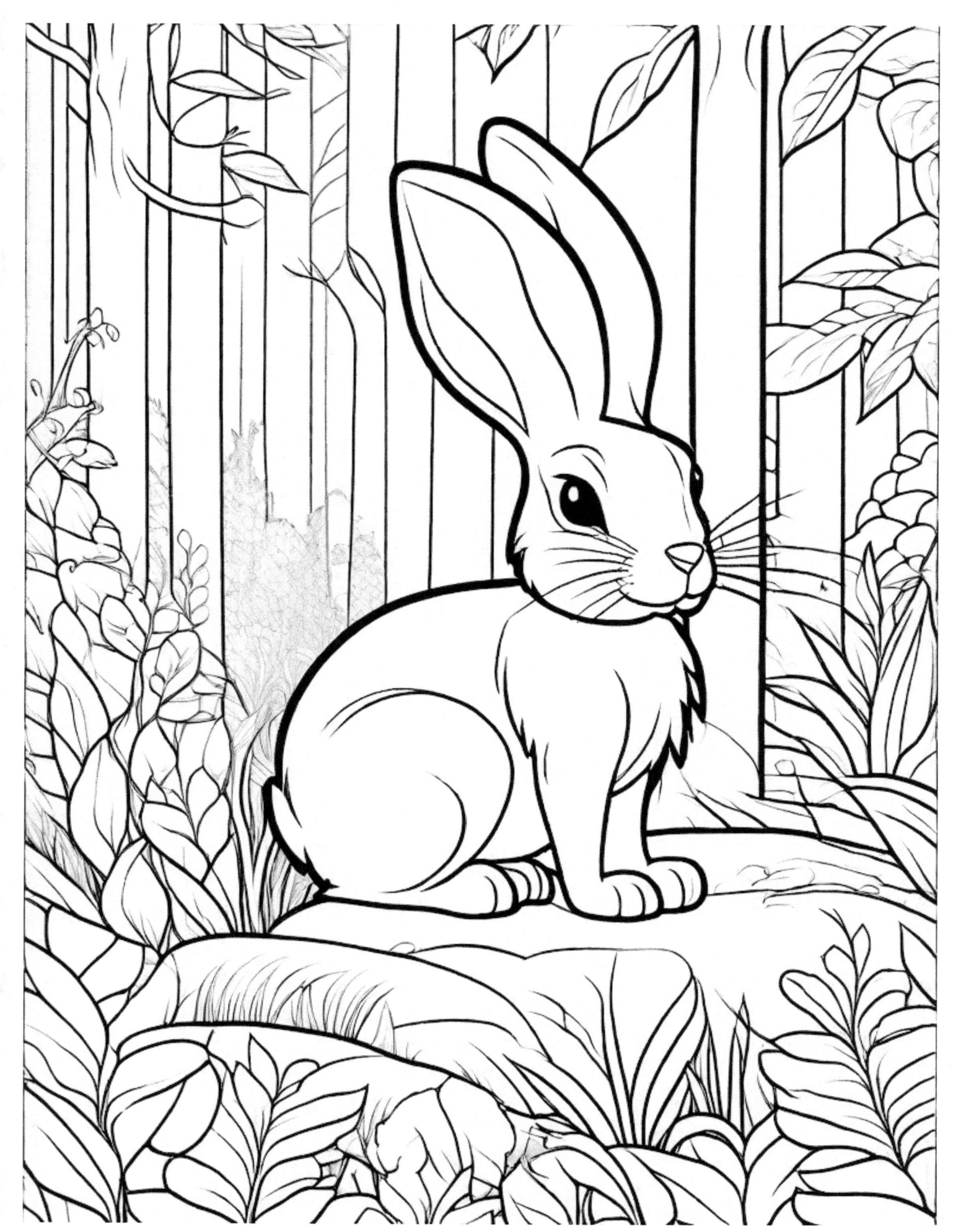

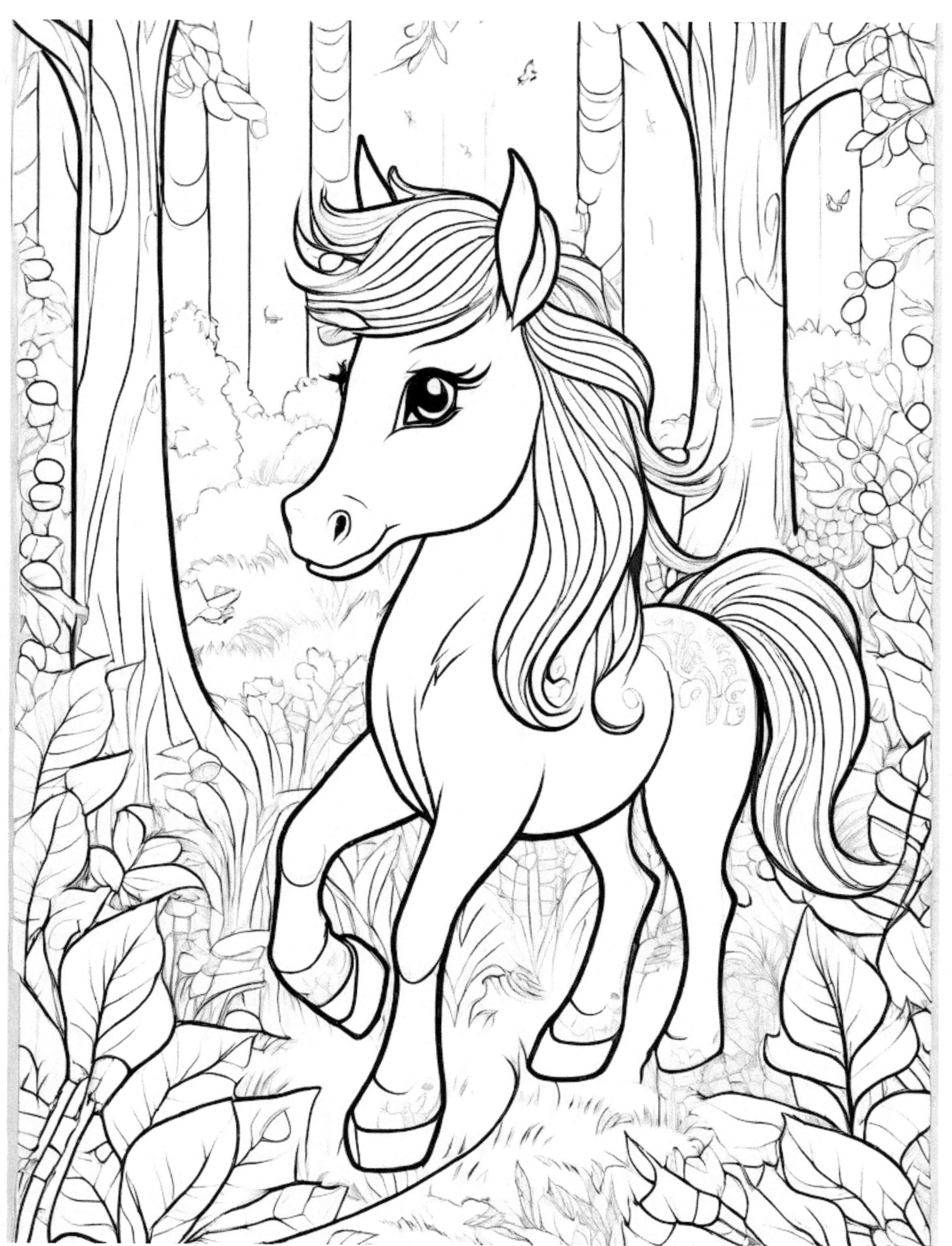

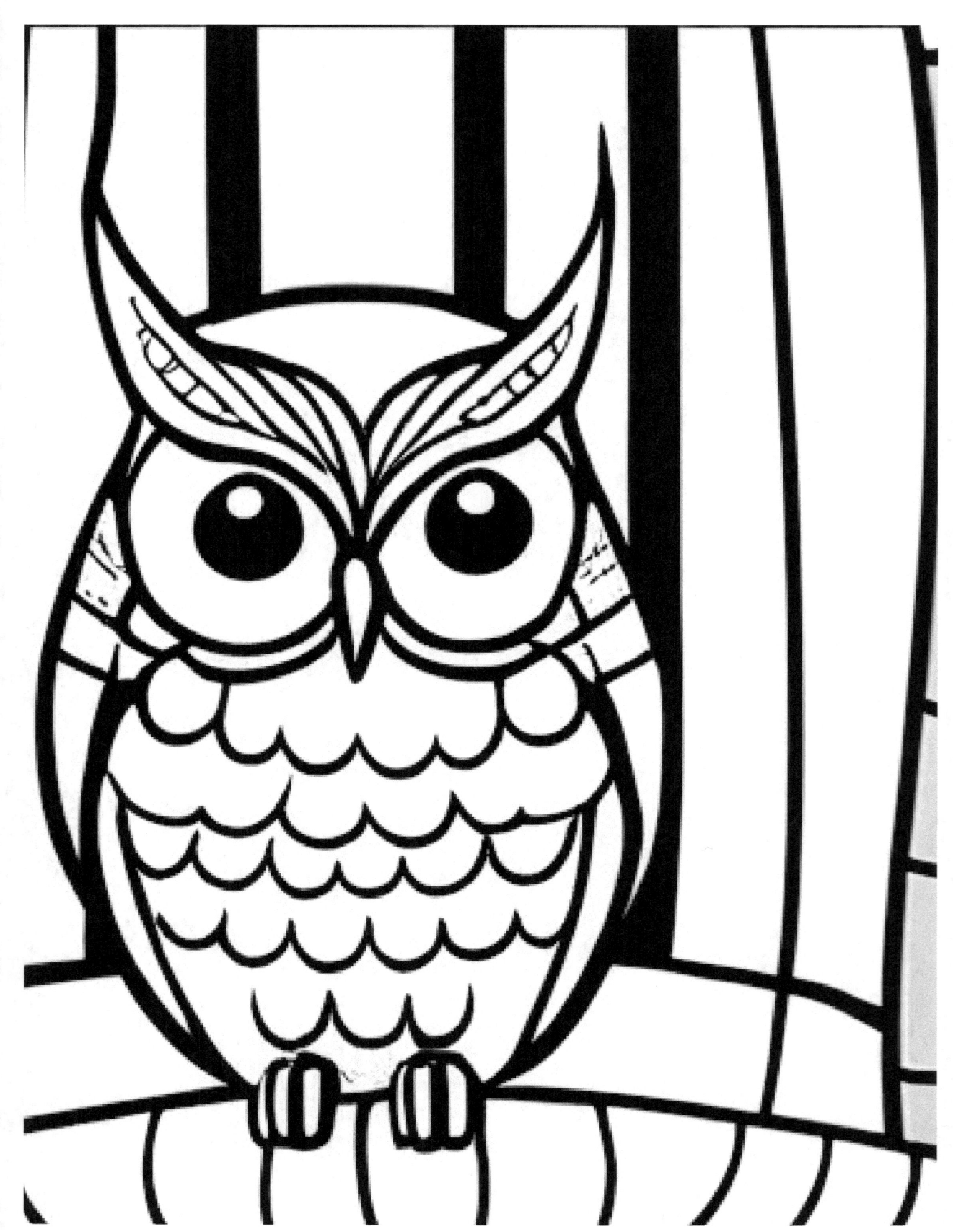

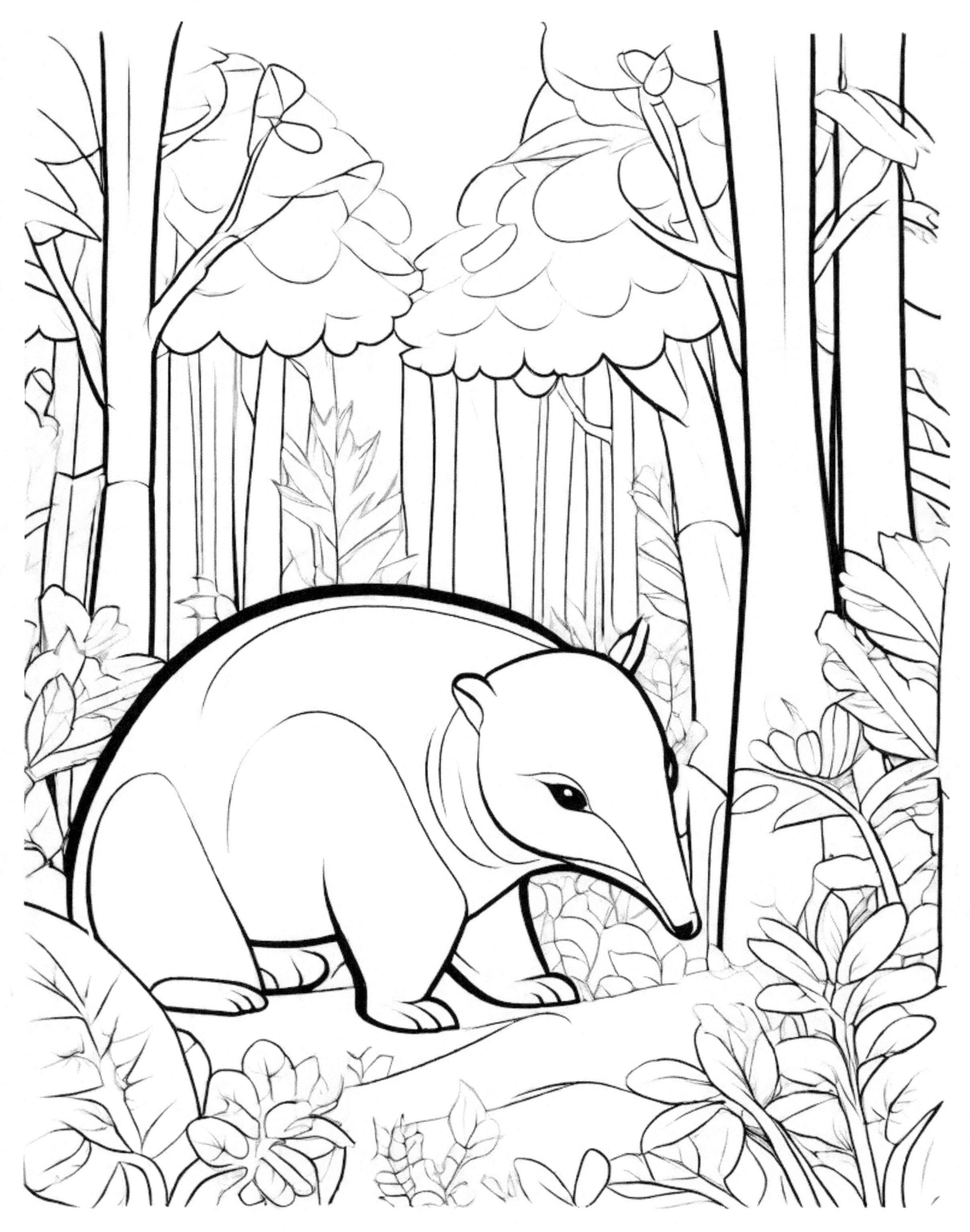

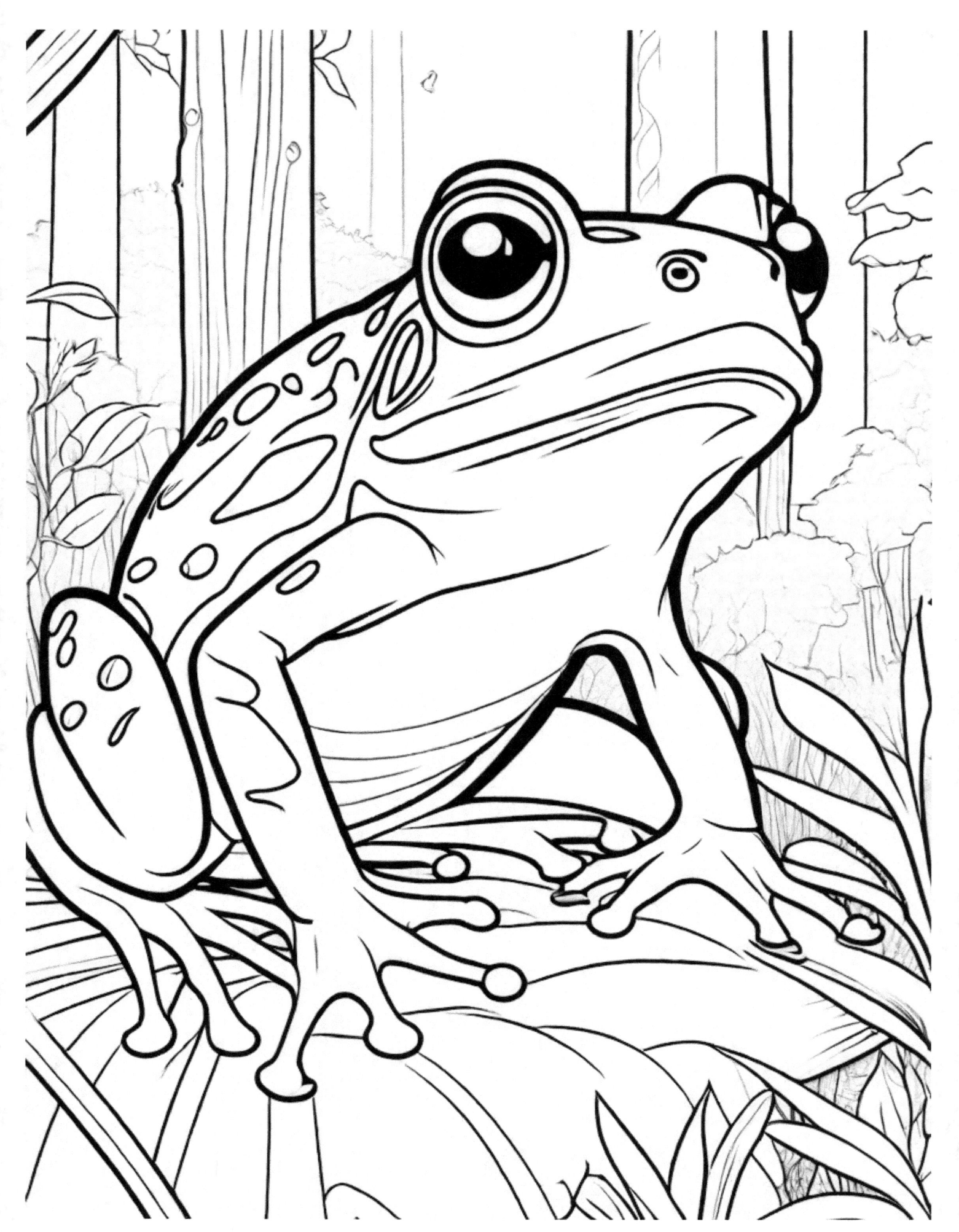

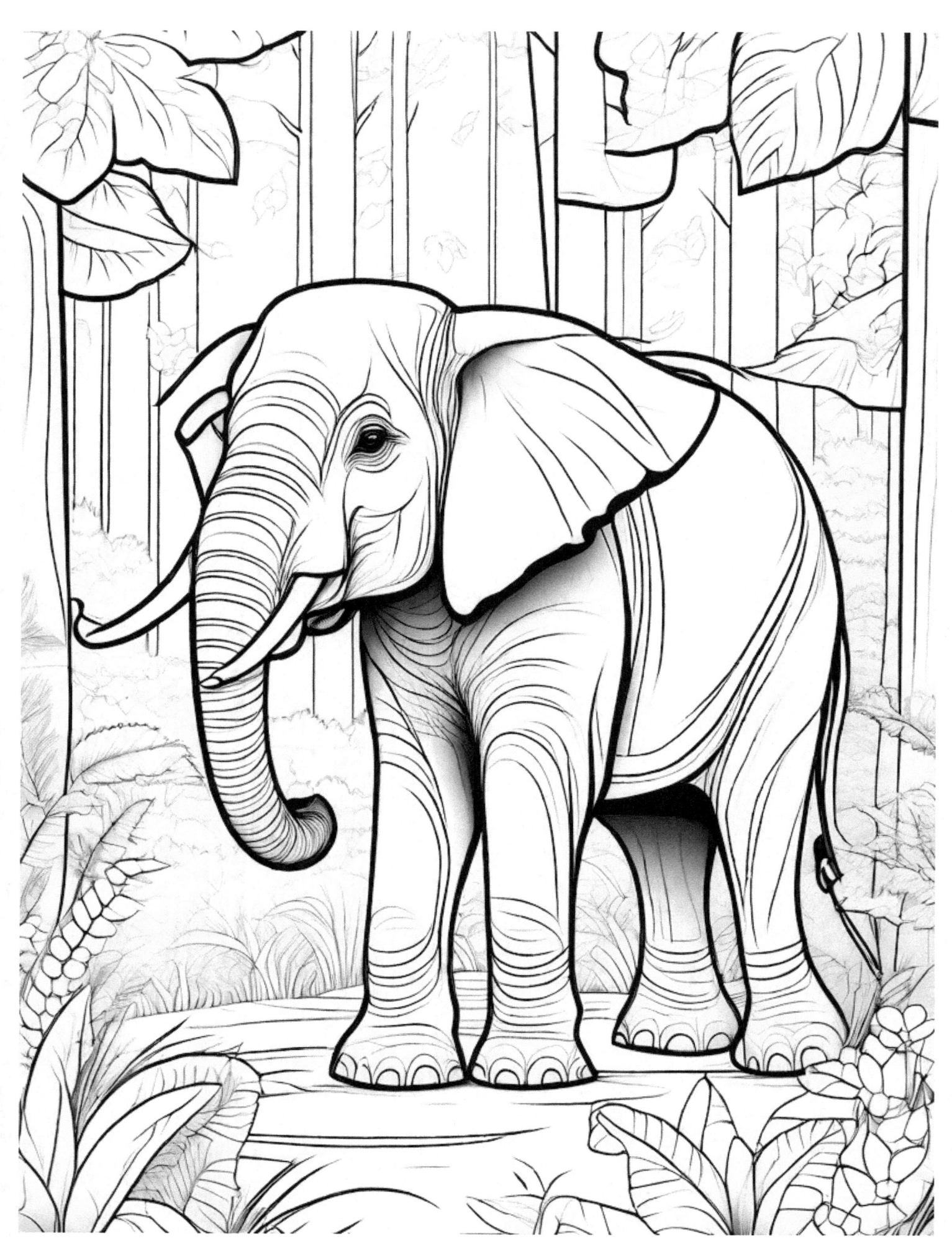

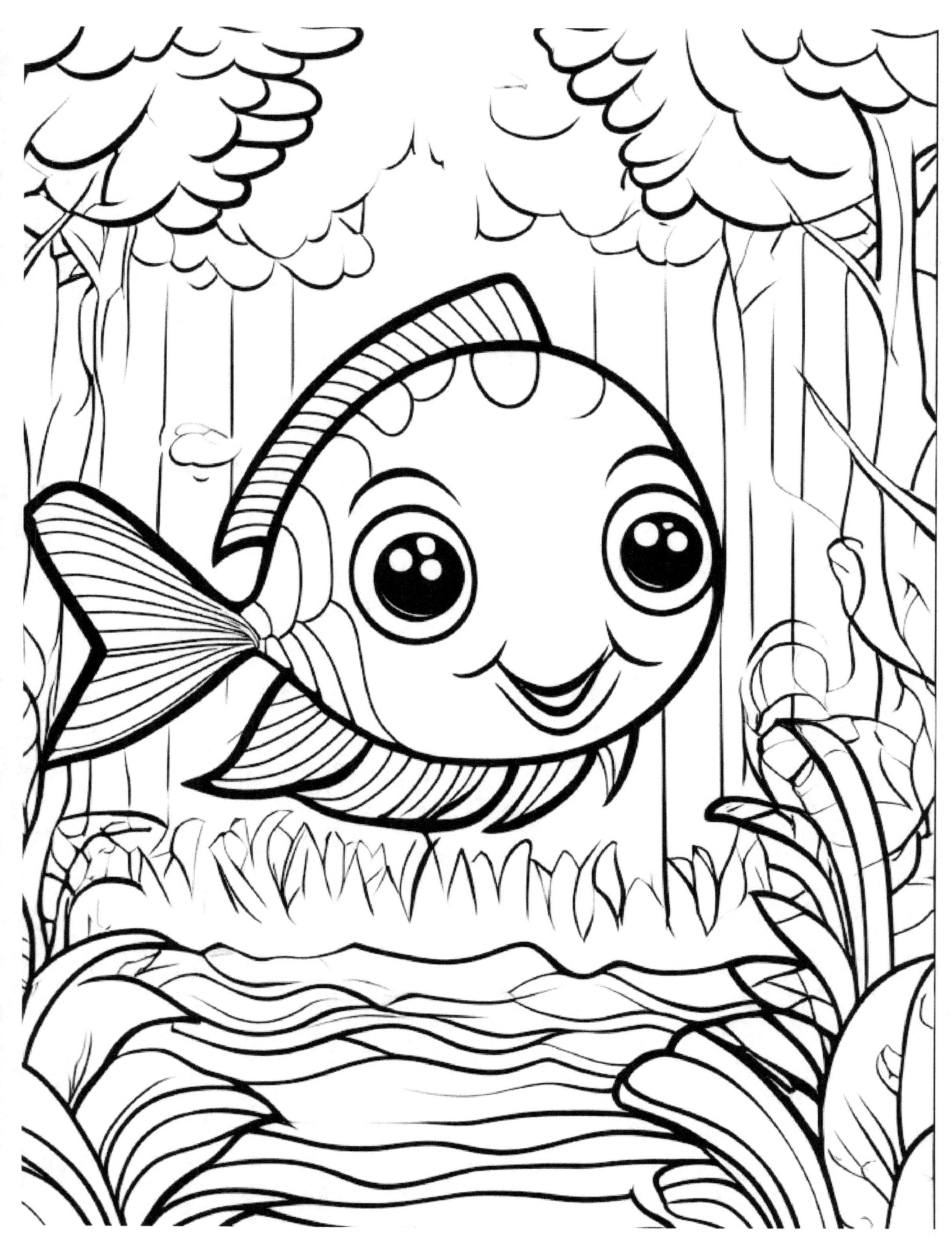

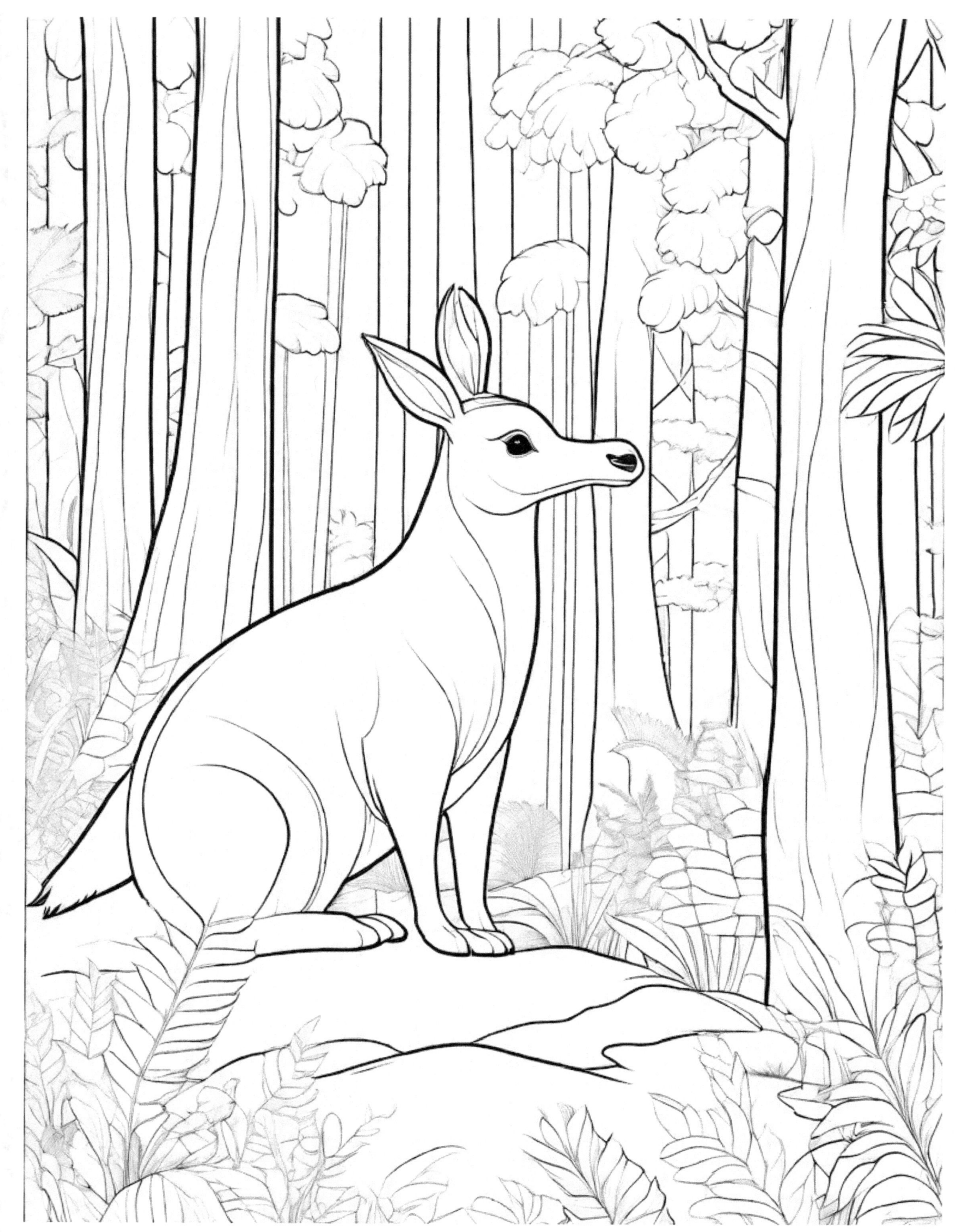

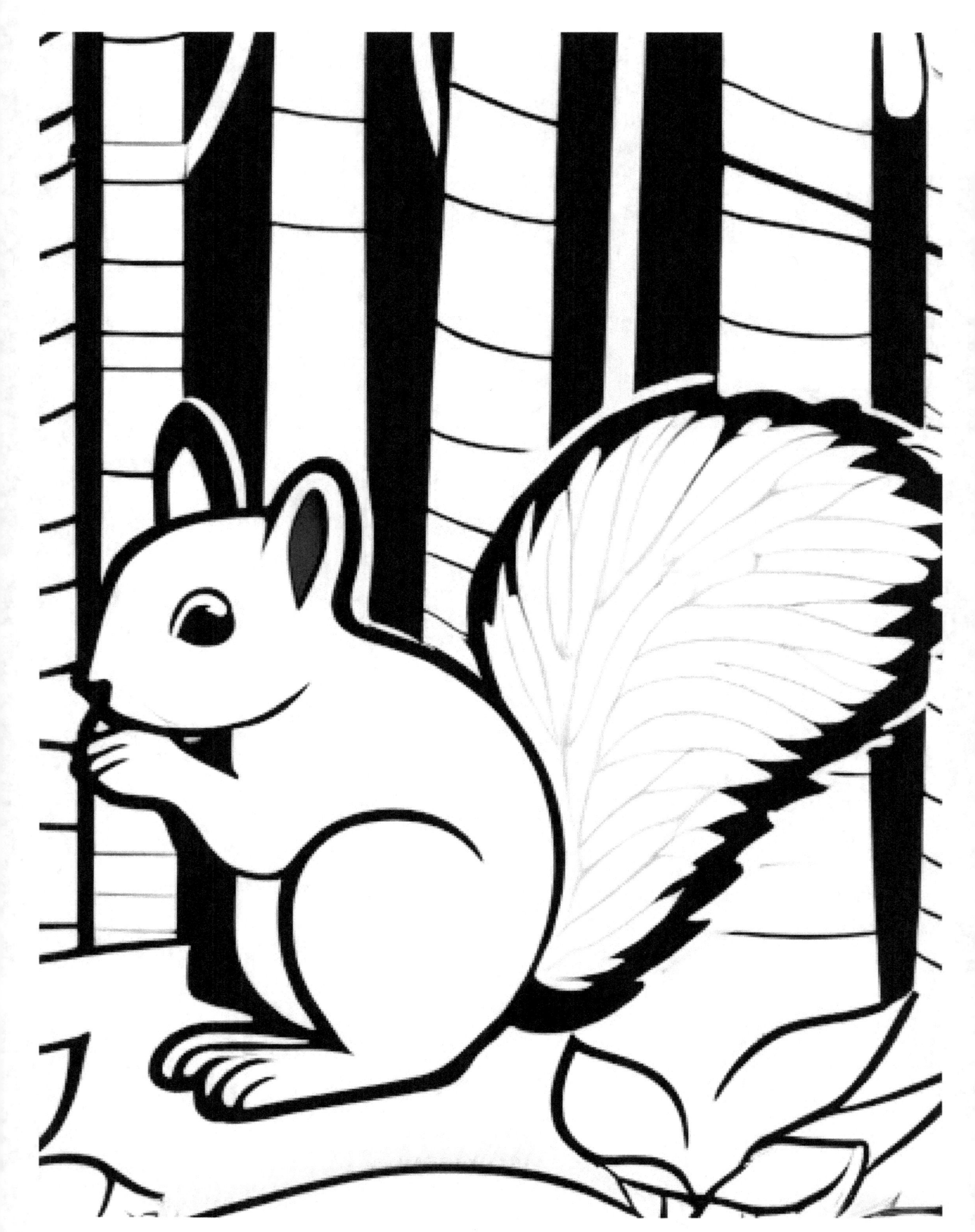

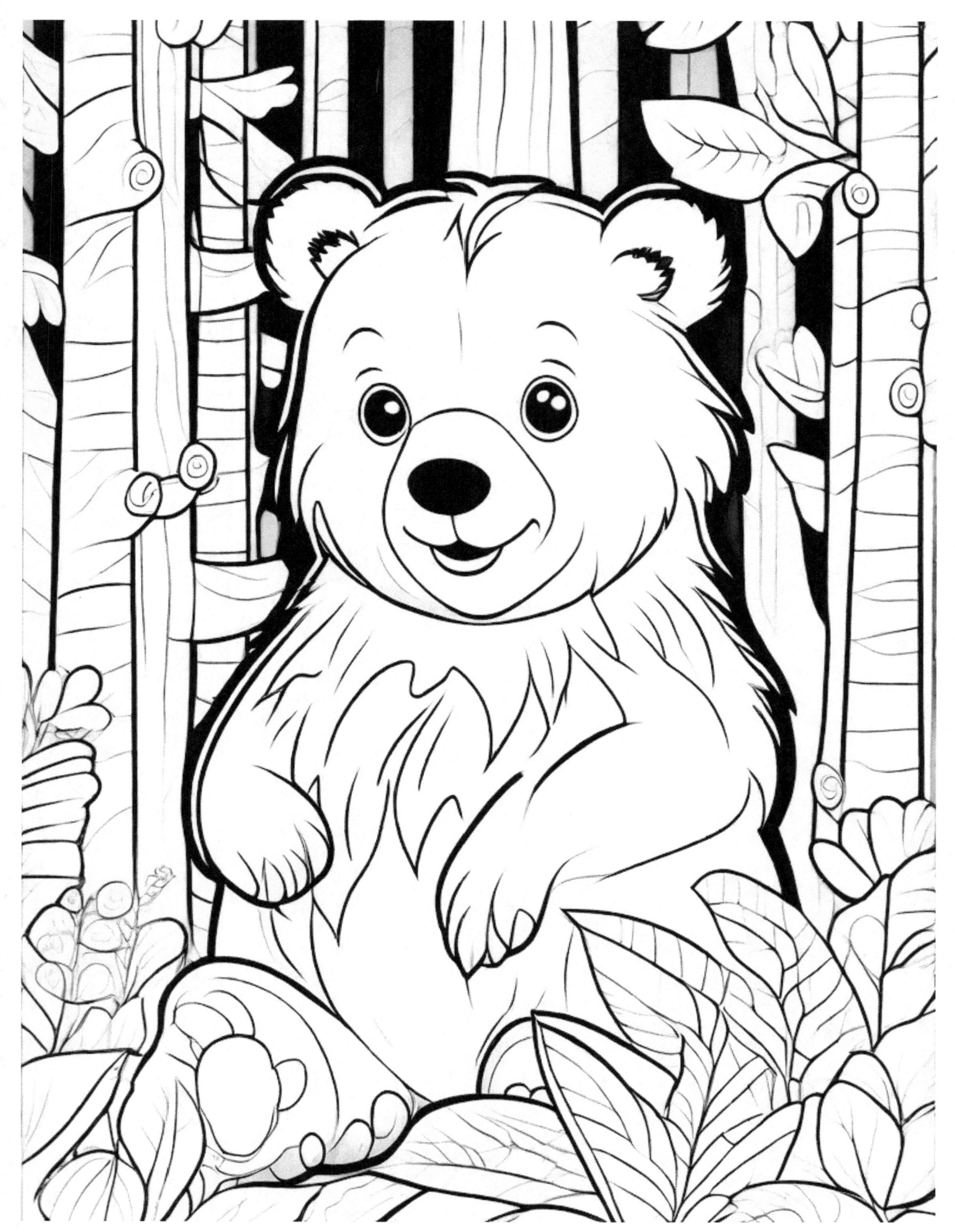

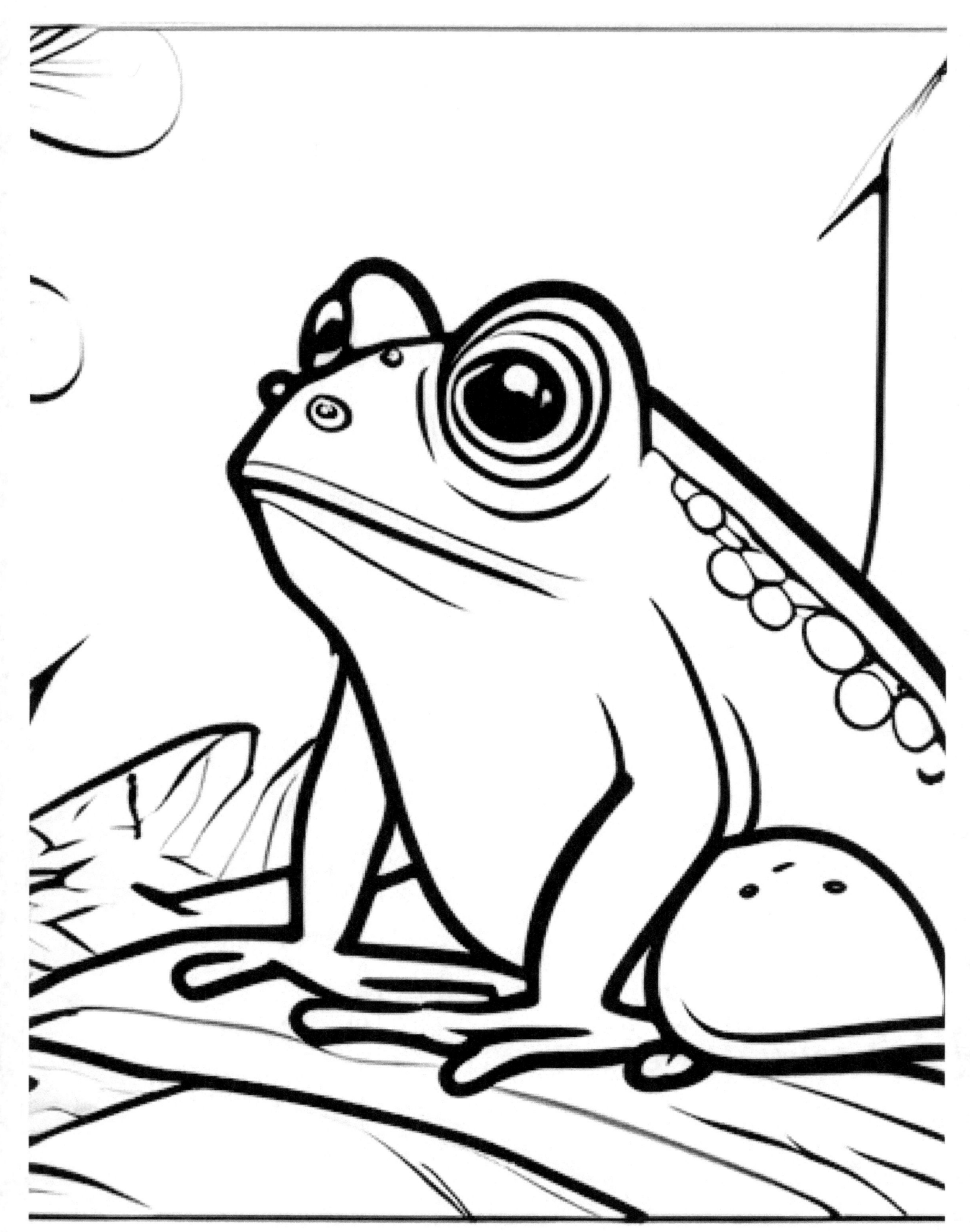

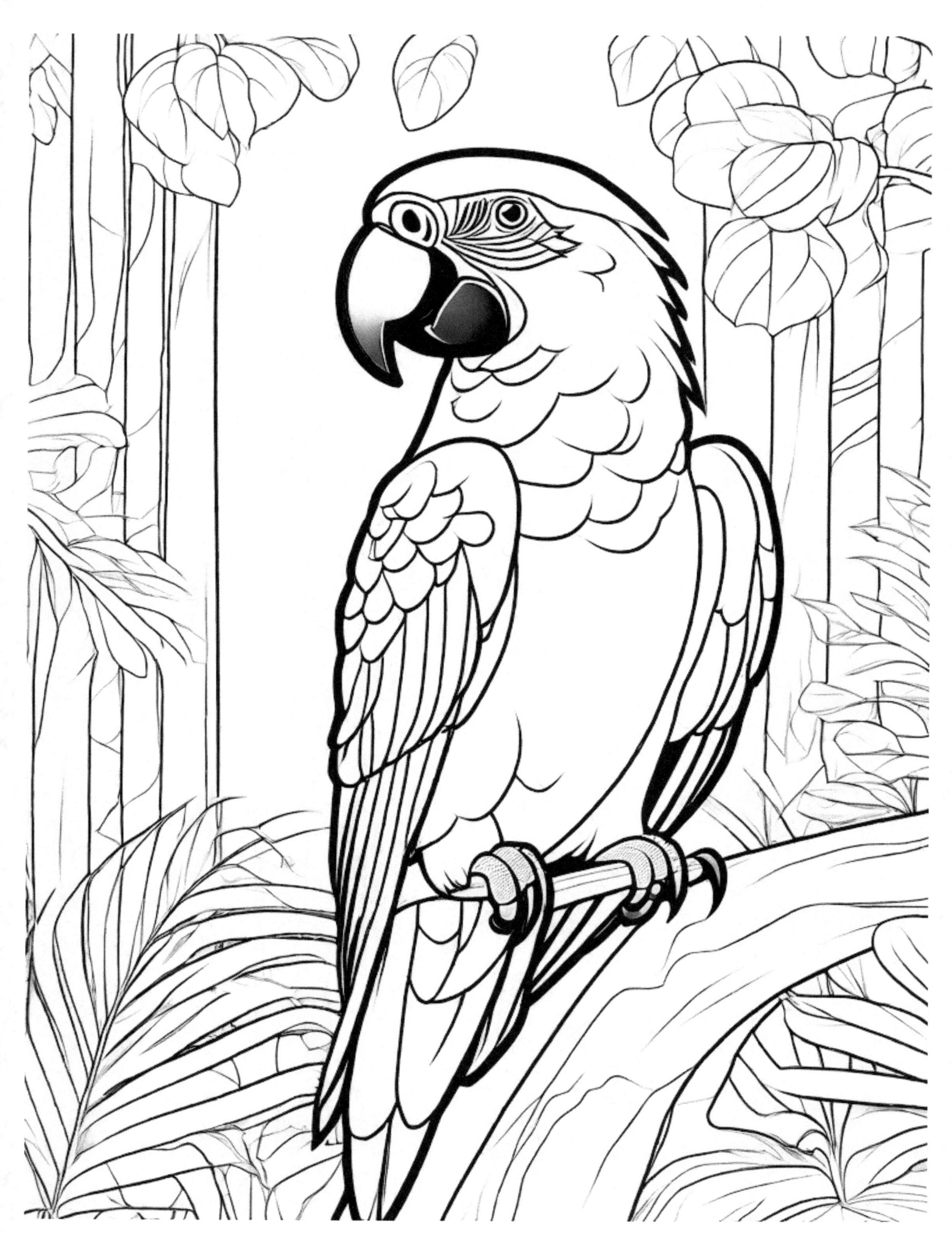

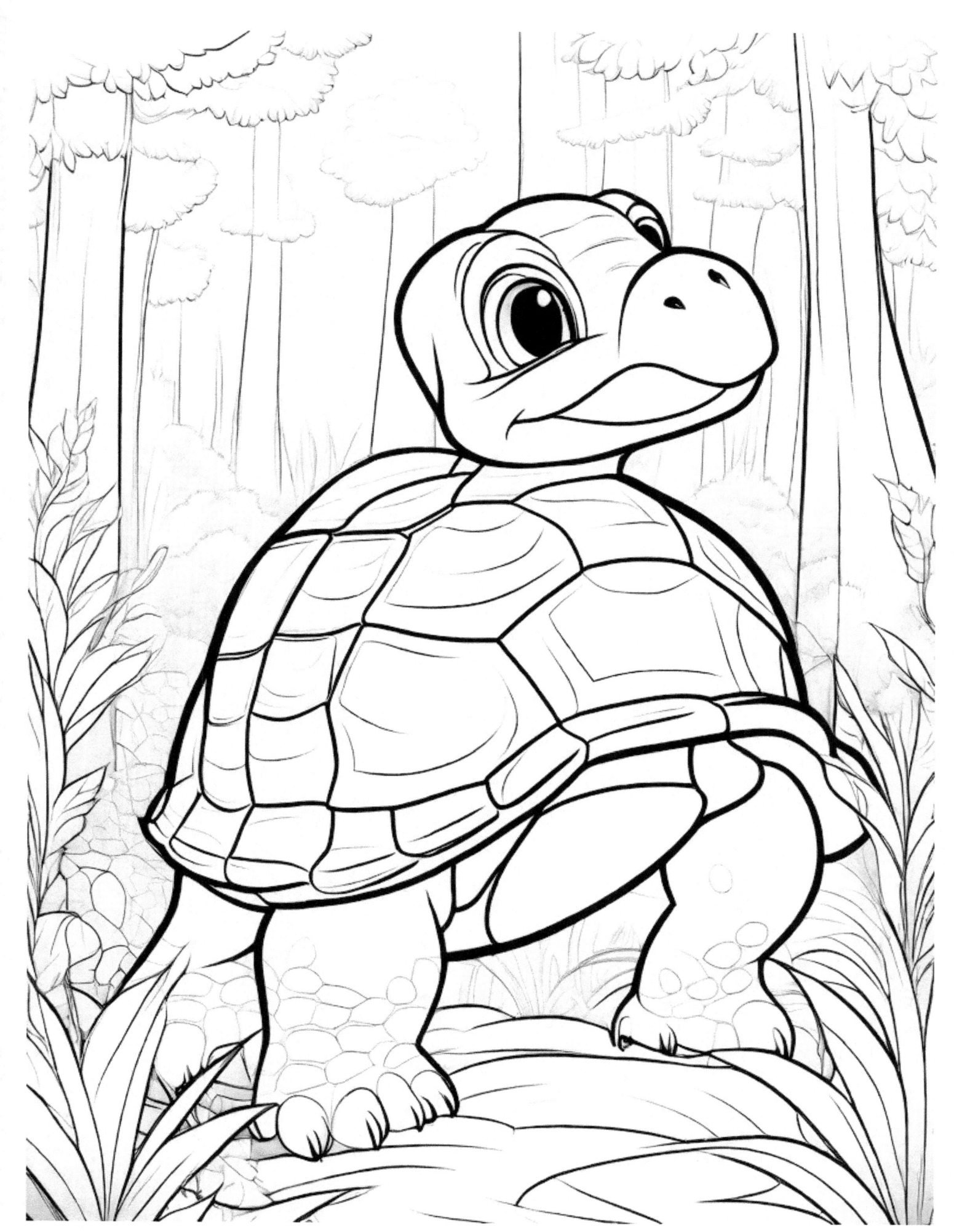

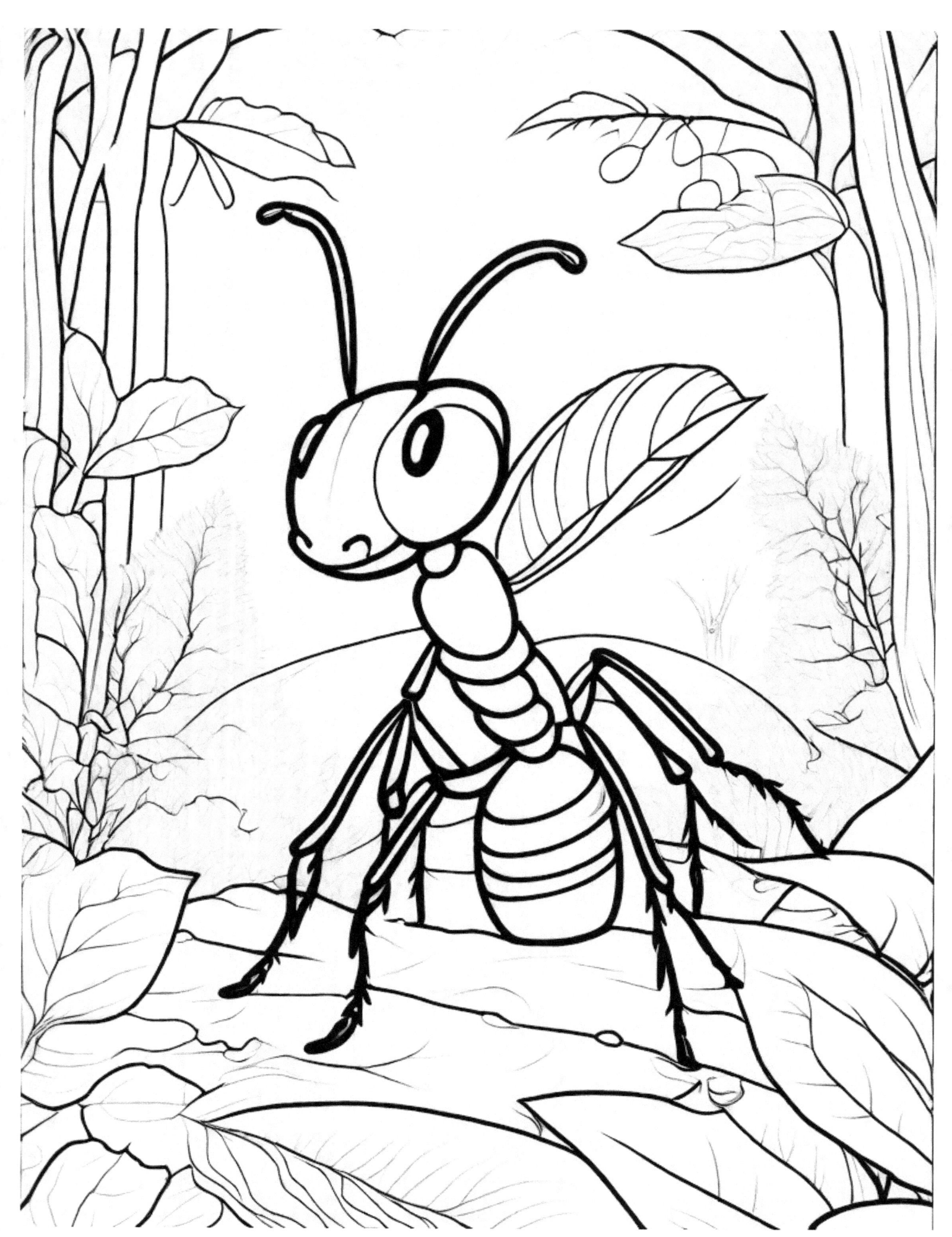

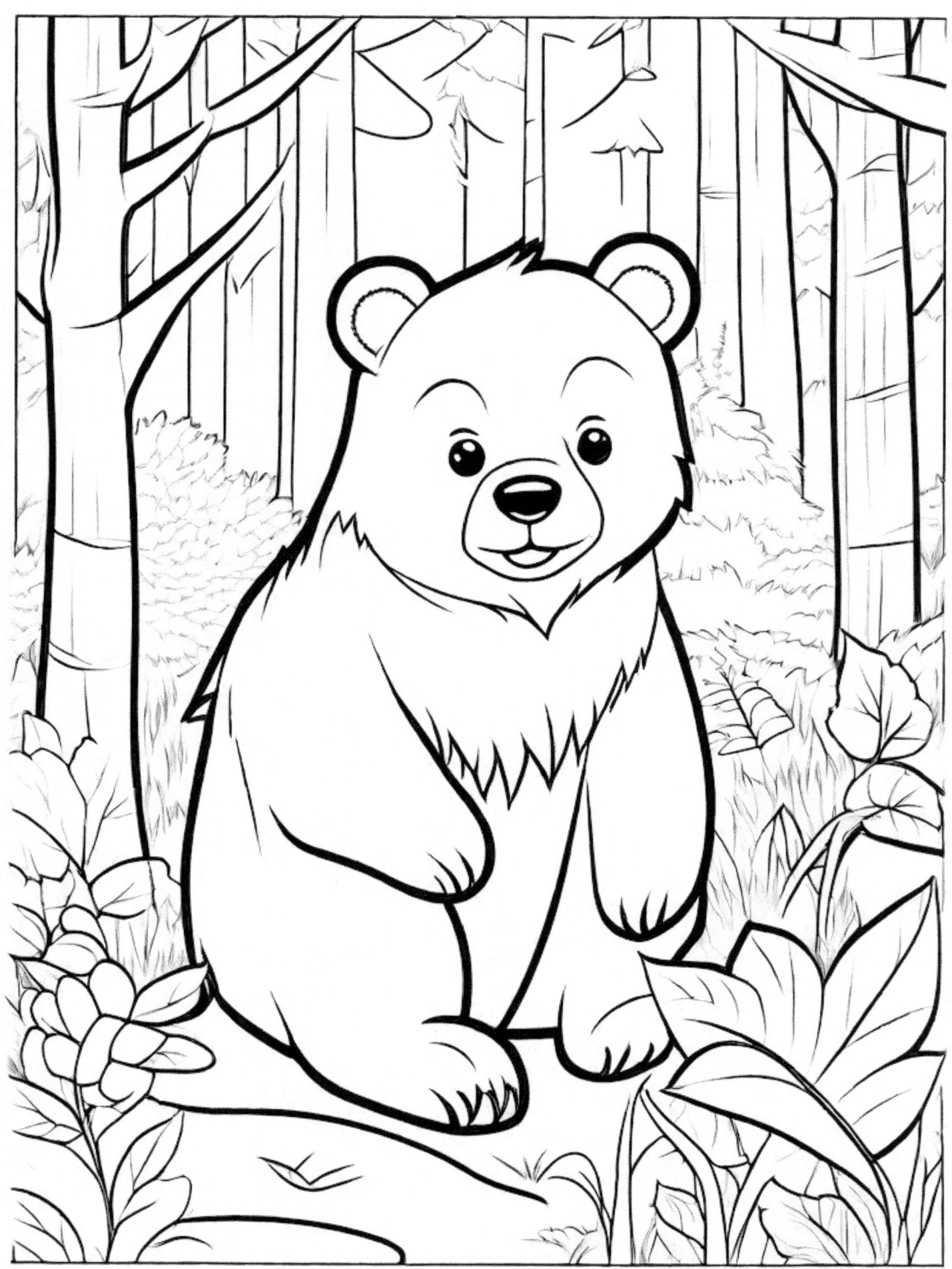

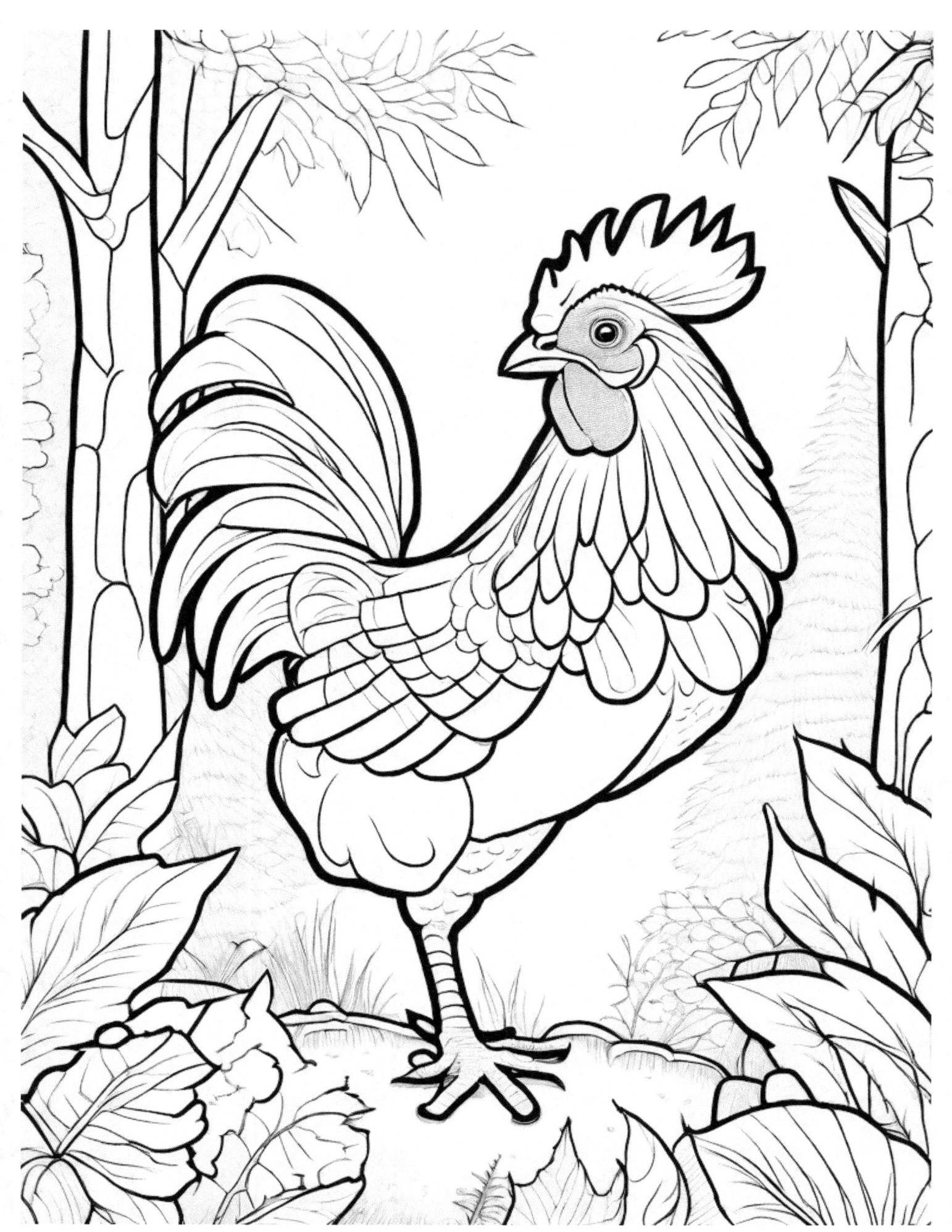

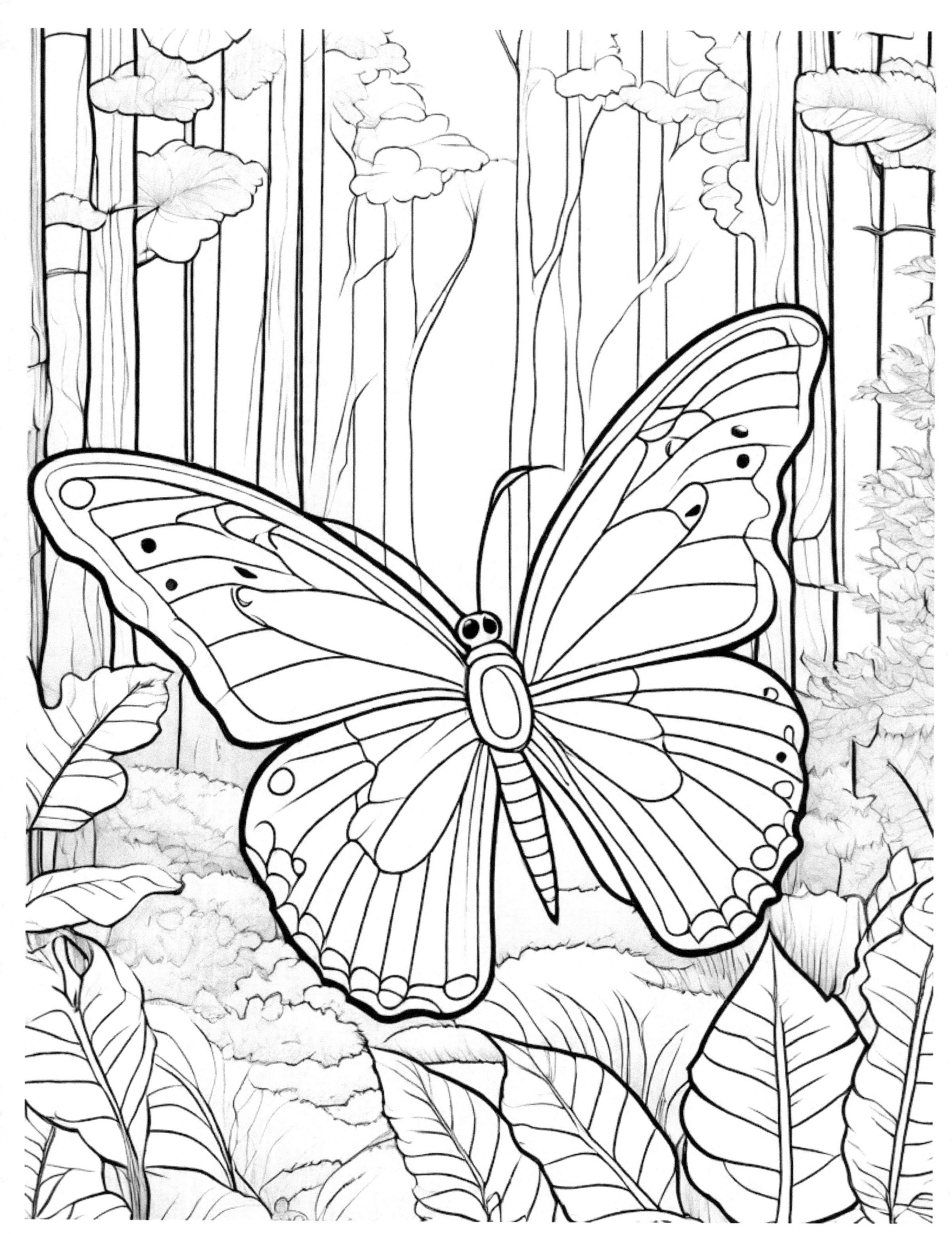

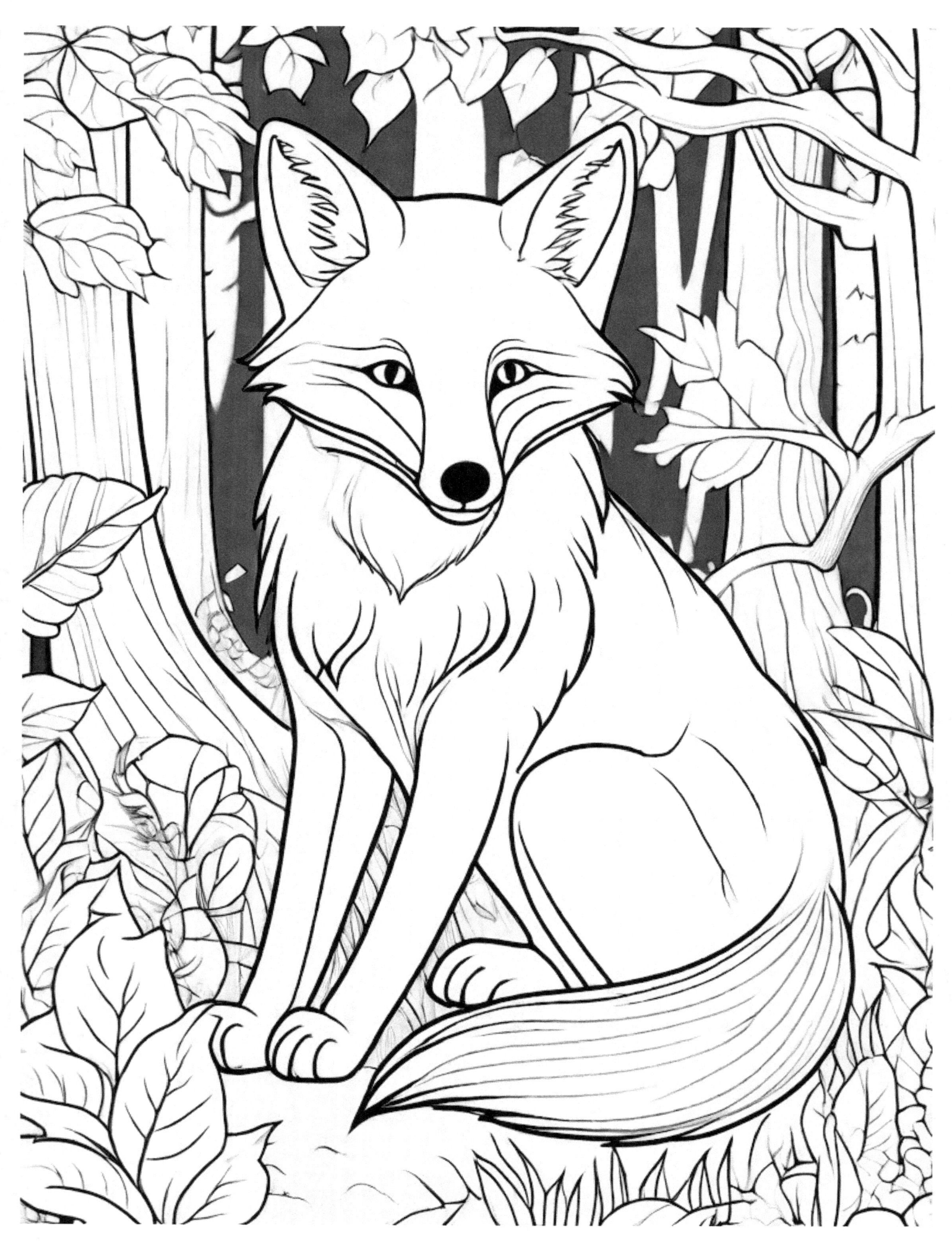

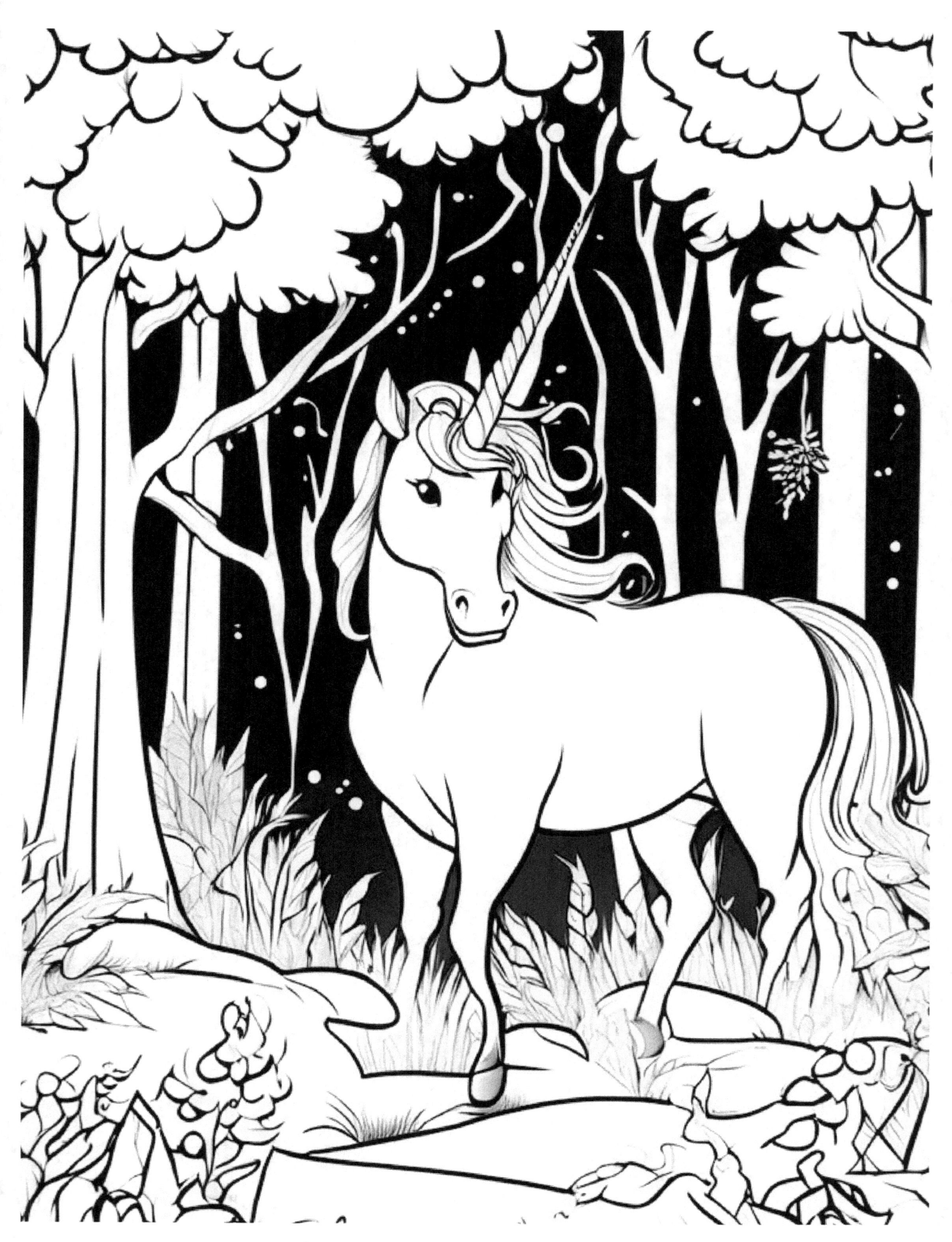

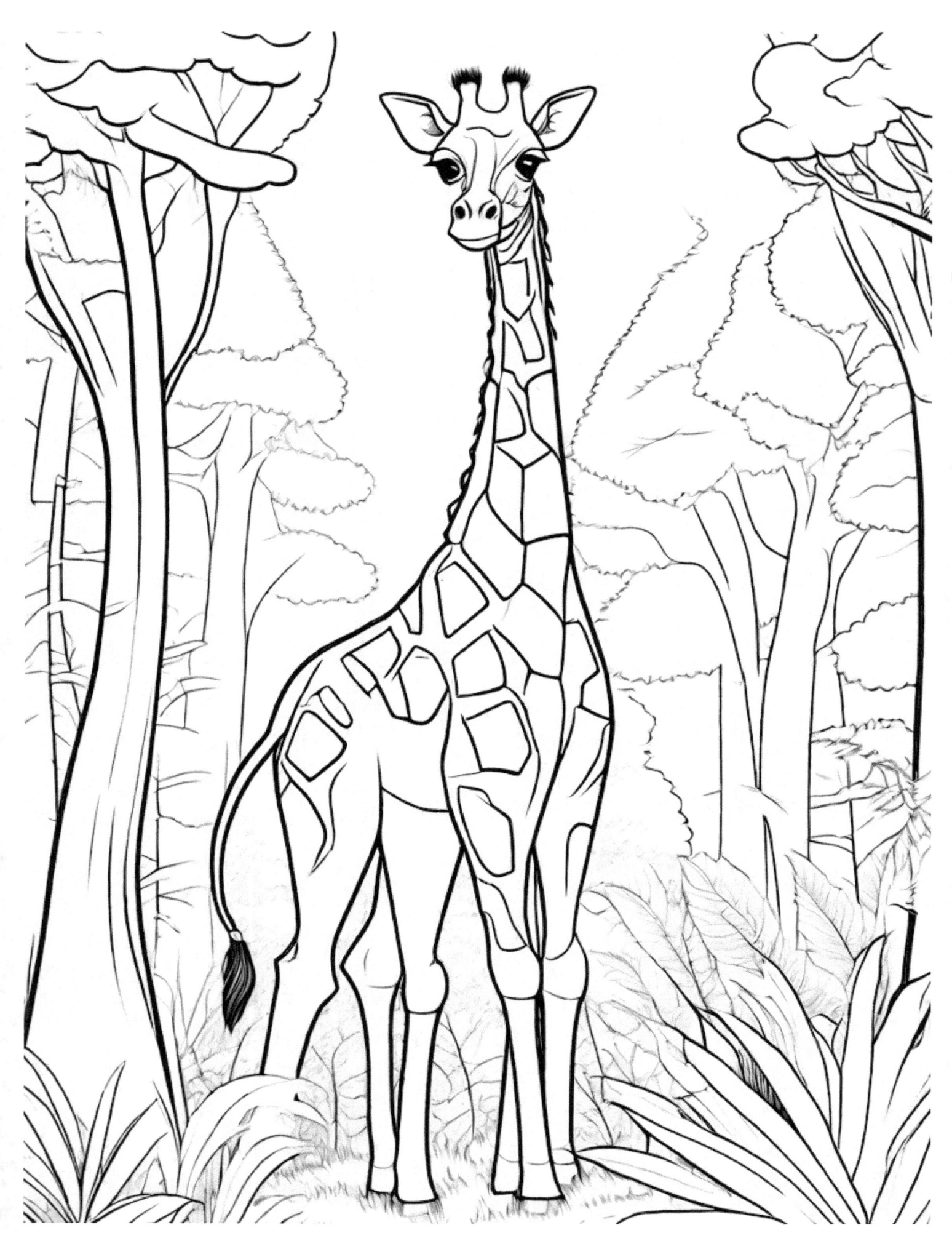

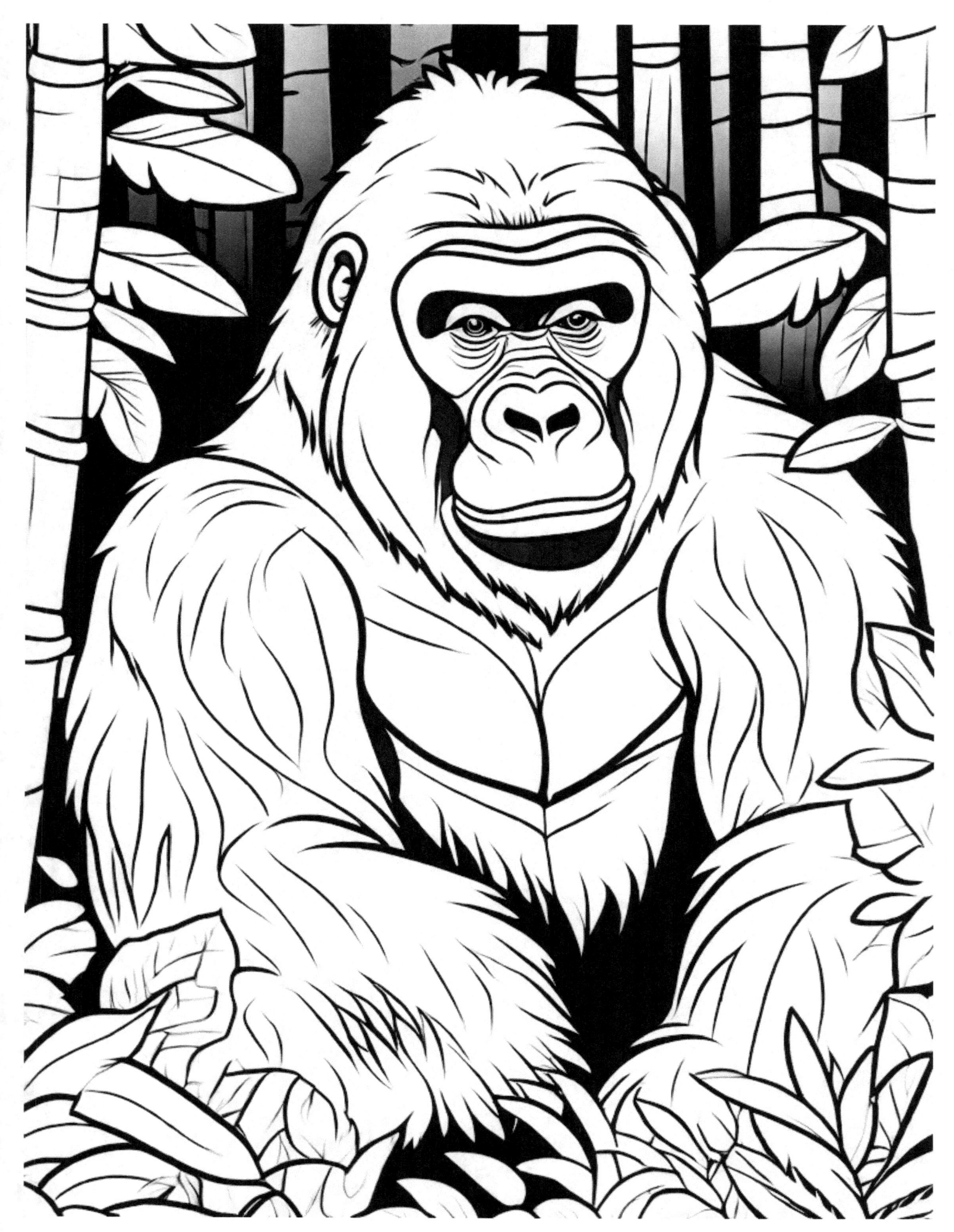

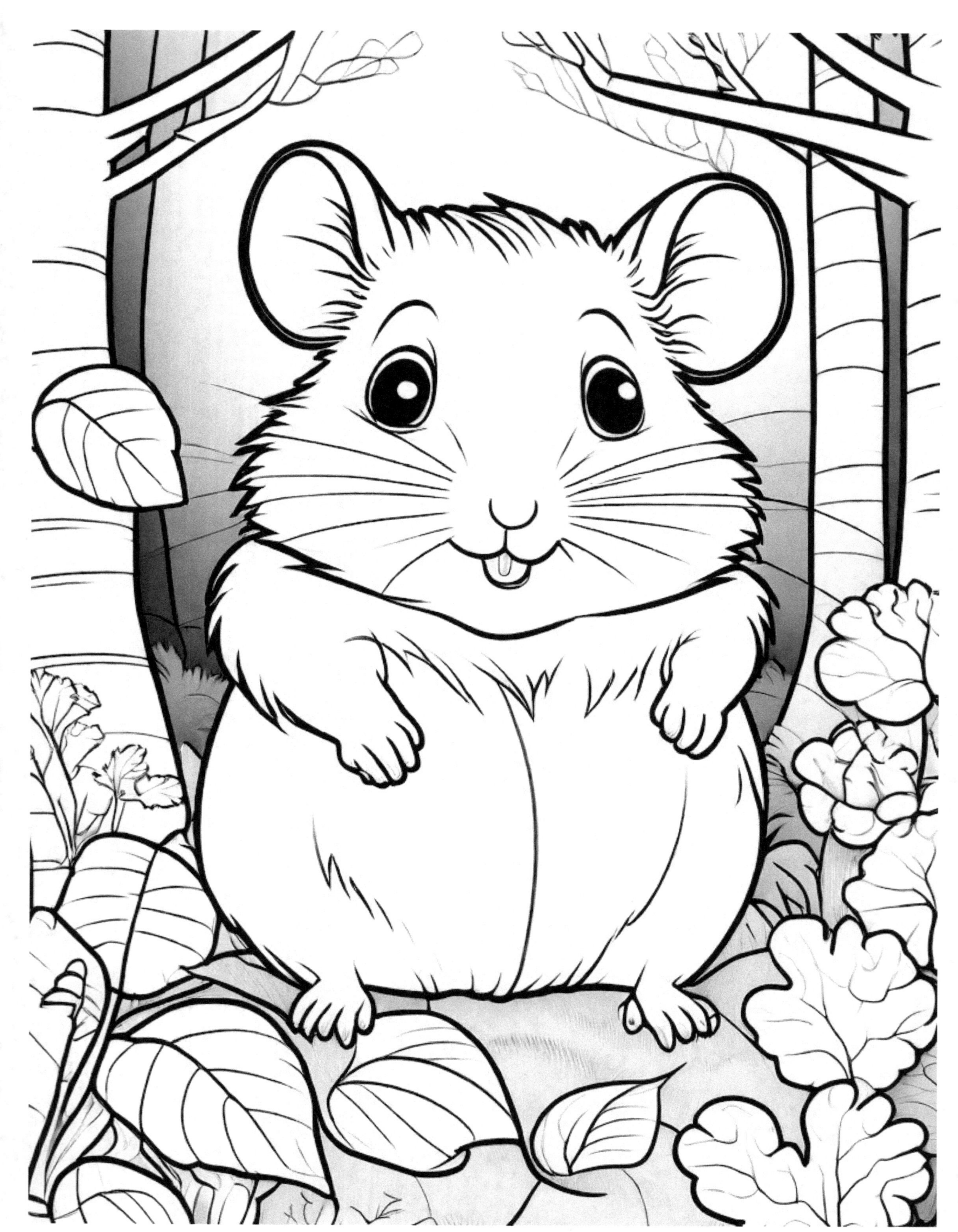

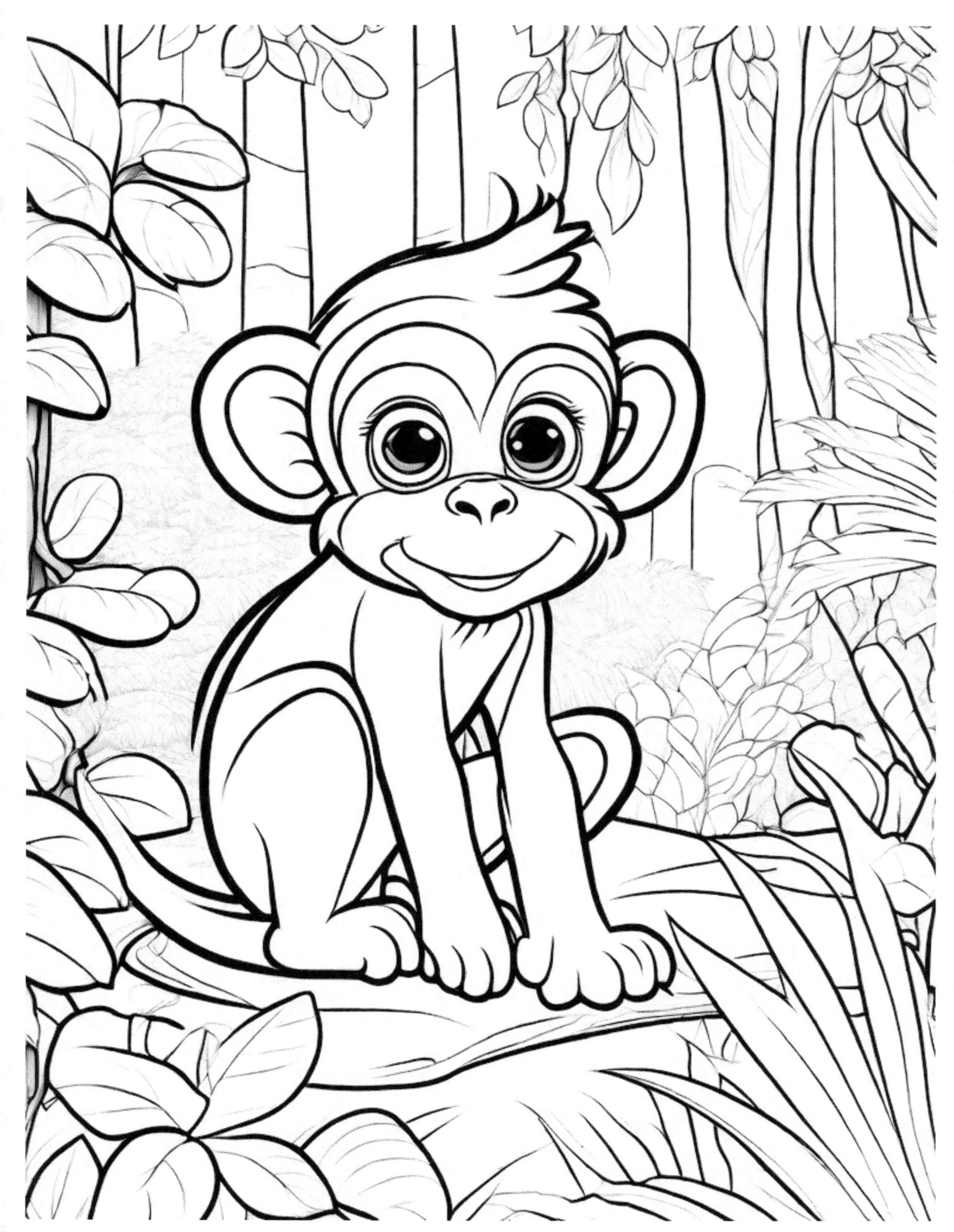

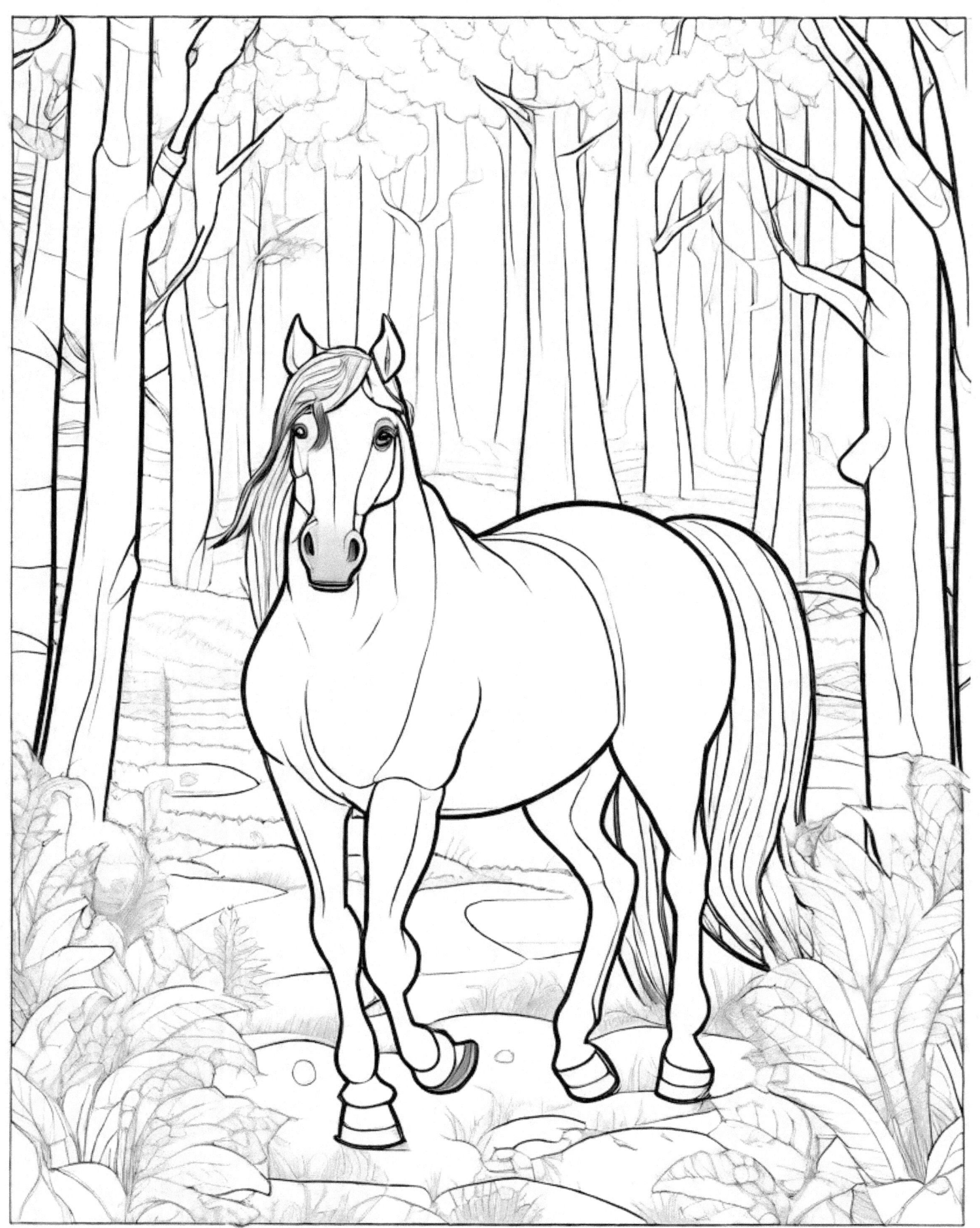

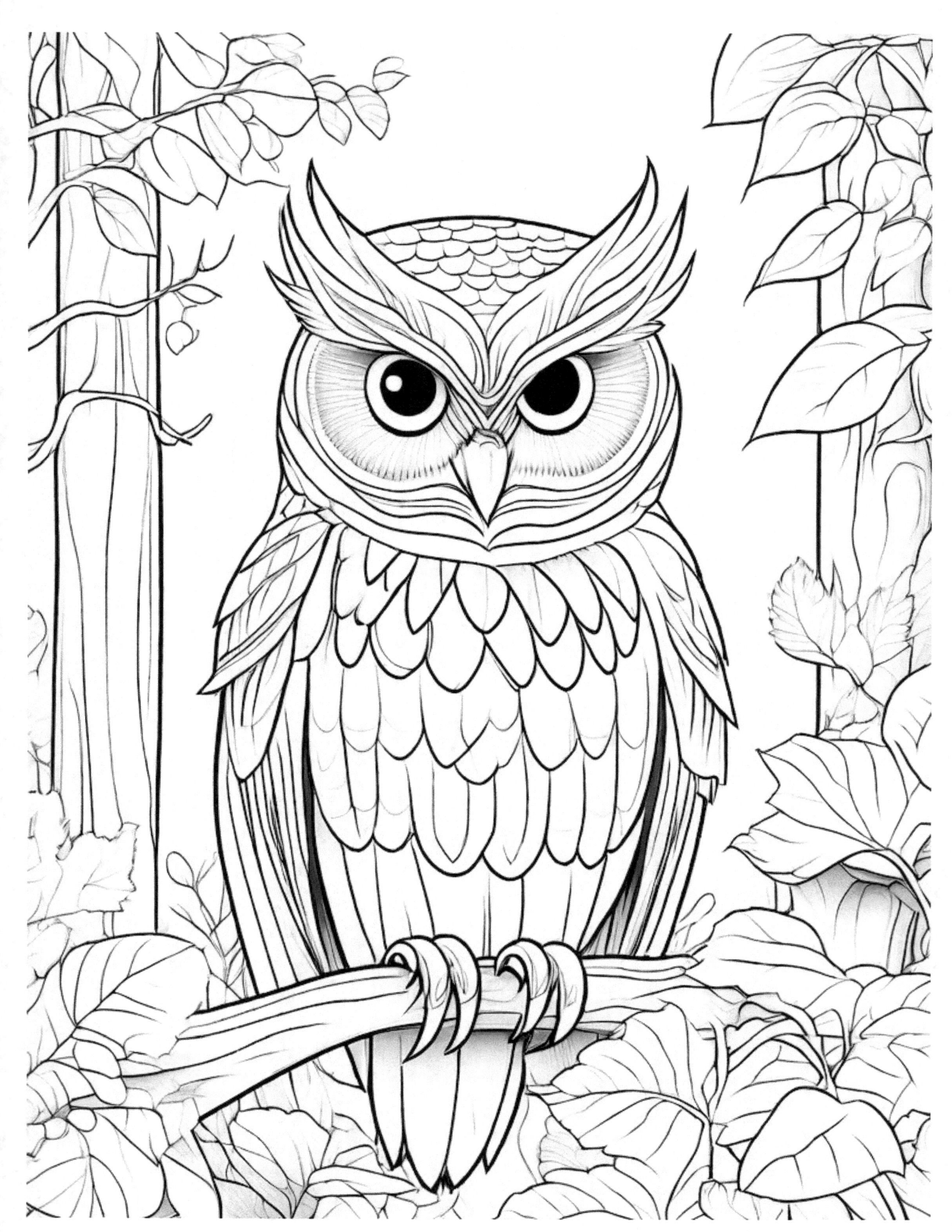

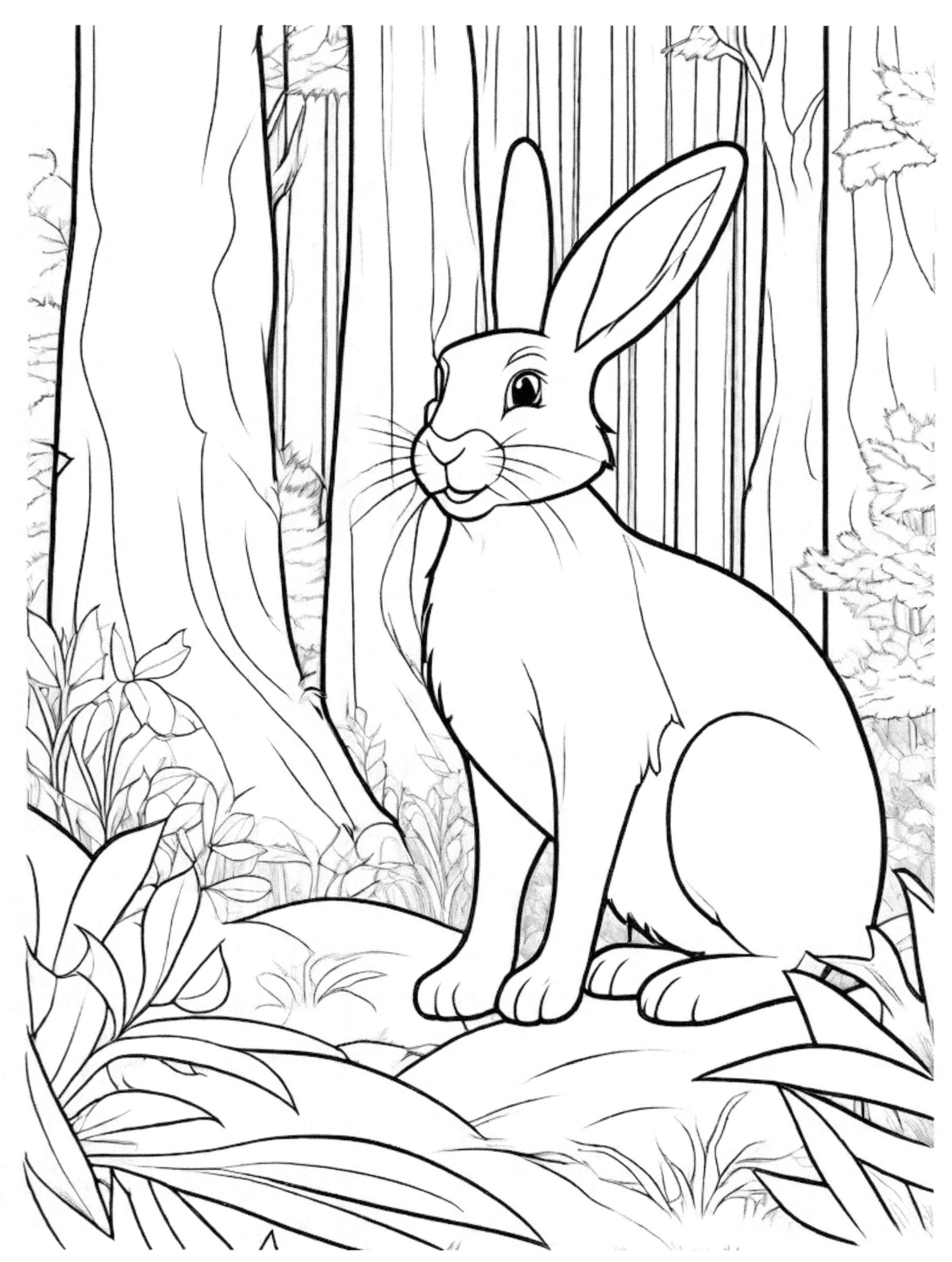

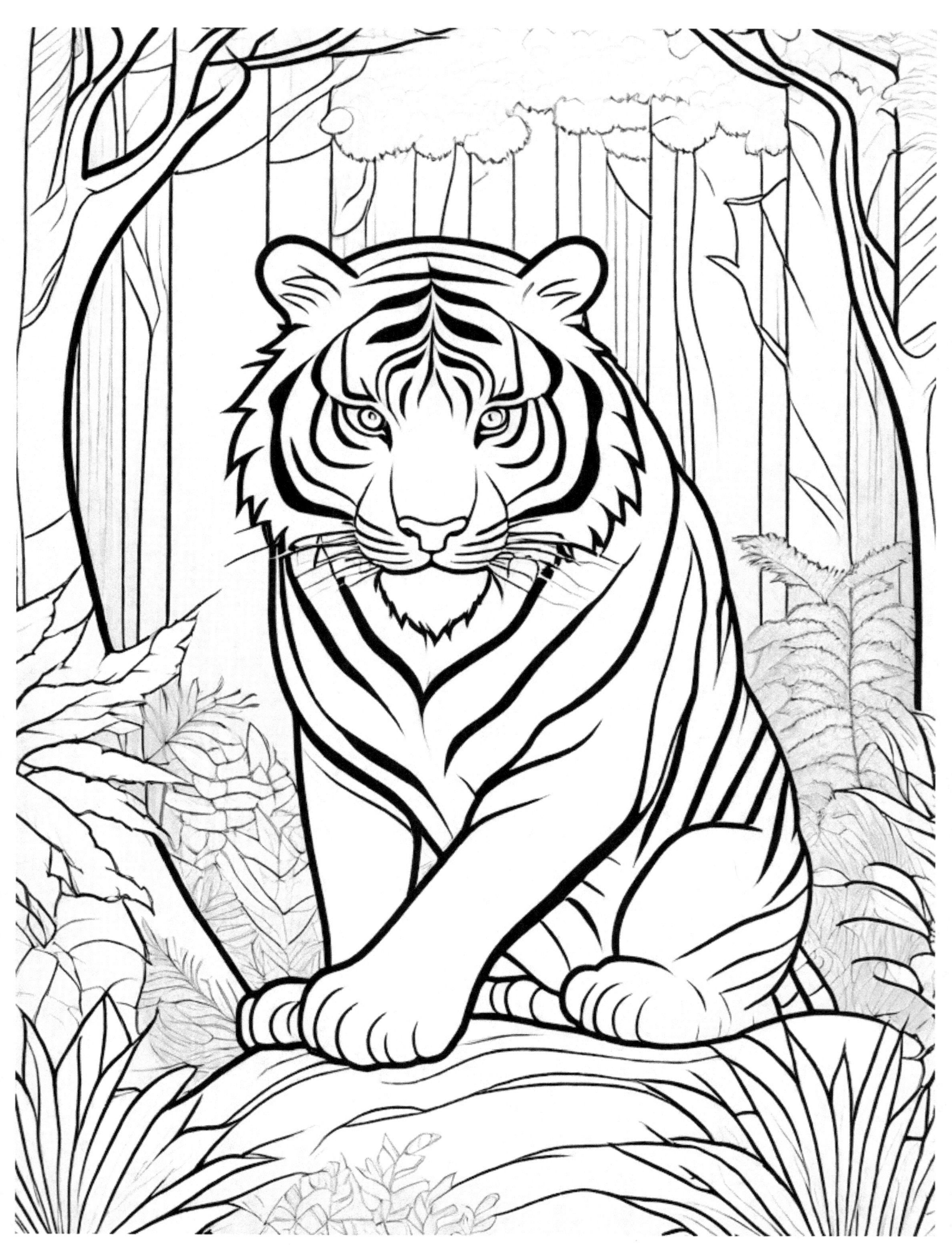

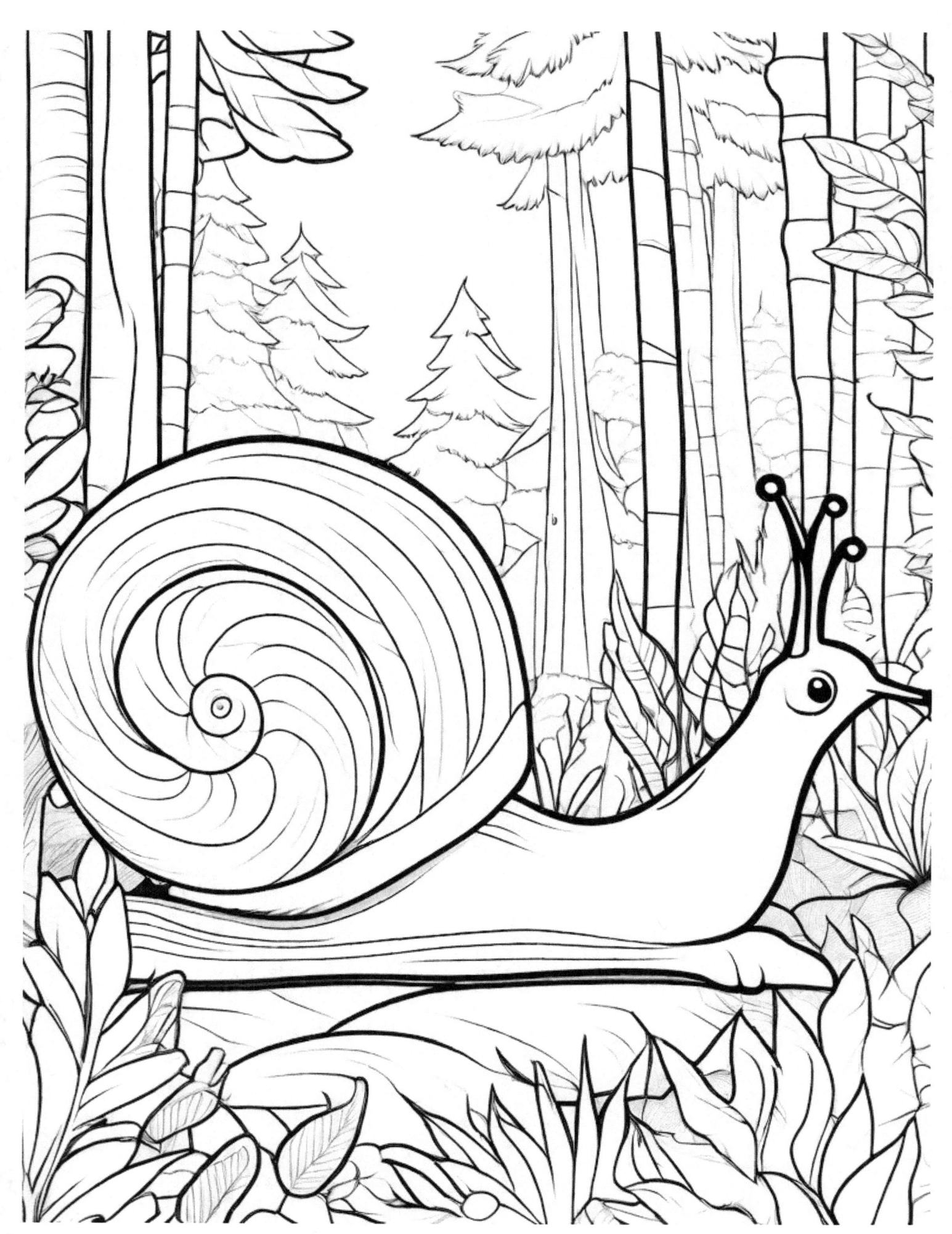

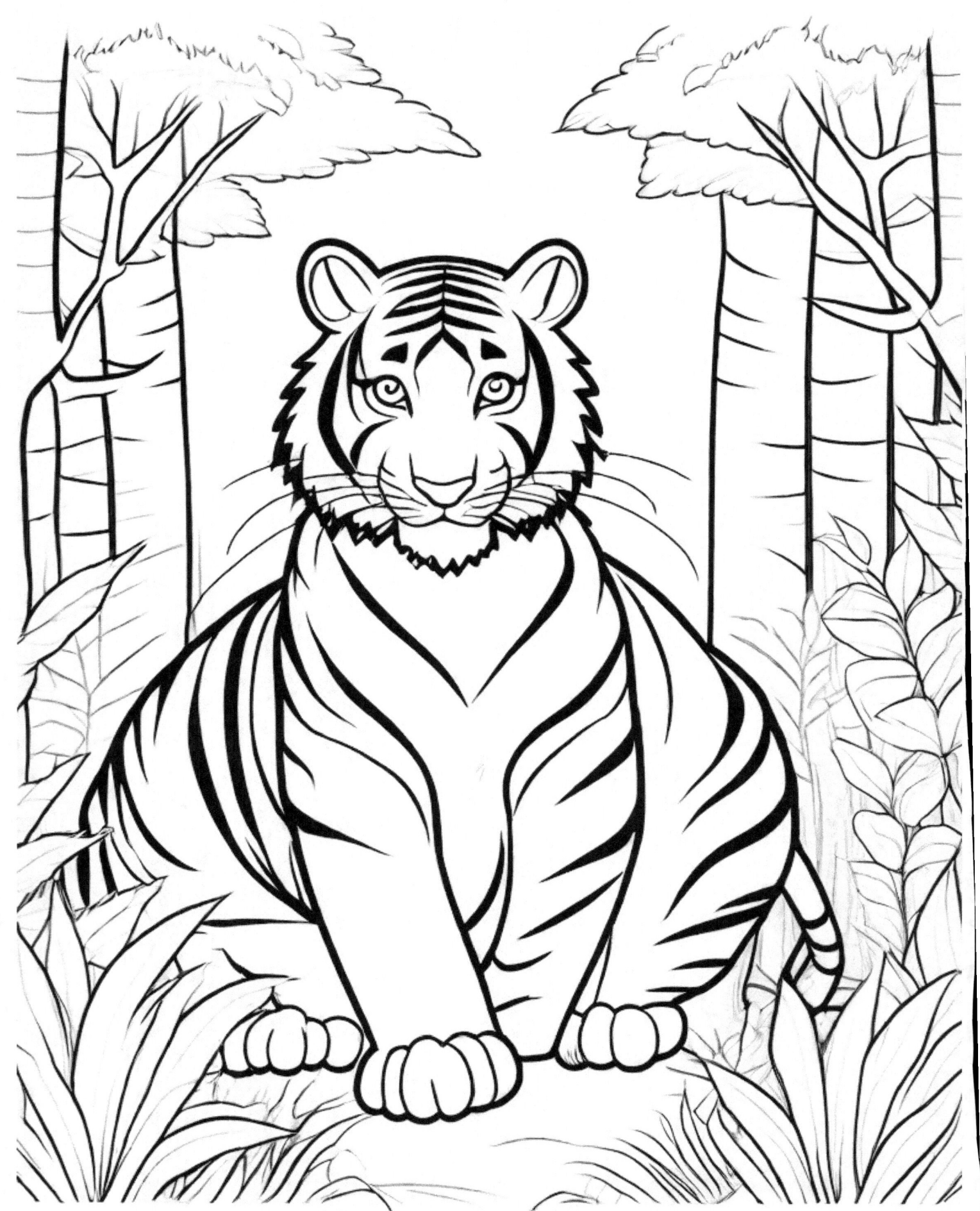

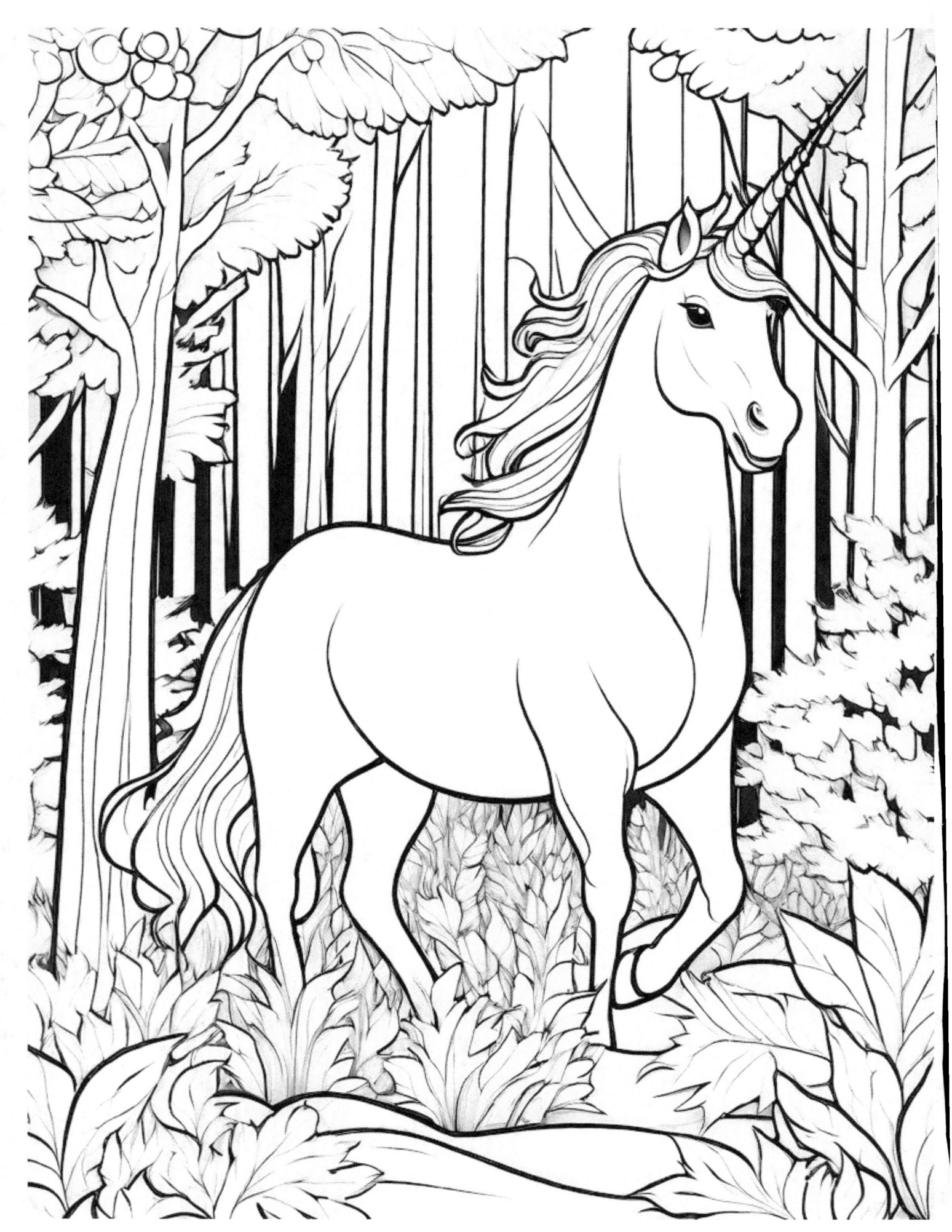

www.ingramcontent.com/pod-product-compliance
Lightning Source LLC
Chambersburg PA
CBHW062120220526
45471CB00010B/3814